POWER BI and Azure

Integrating Cloud Analytics for Scalable Solutions

Kiet Huynh

Table of Contents

Introduction

1.1 The Convergence of Power BI and Azure

The Role of Cloud Analytics

In the world of data analytics, the role of cloud analytics cannot be overstated. It's a game-changer for organizations of all sizes. Imagine a retail chain operating in multiple locations. They need real-time insights into their sales, inventory, and customer data. In a traditional on-premises setup, accessing and processing this data in real-time across all locations would be a monumental challenge. Cloud analytics changes this dynamic.

With cloud analytics, the retail chain can ingest data from all its stores, process it in the cloud, and provide actionable insights in real-time. For example, during a sales promotion, the system can instantly track sales trends across stores, helping the chain optimize stock levels and tailor marketing efforts. This agility is only possible with cloud analytics.

The Synergy of Power BI and Azure

Now, let's delve into the synergy of Power BI and Azure. Power BI, as a powerful business intelligence tool, is adept at turning data into visually compelling insights. Azure, Microsoft's cloud platform, provides the infrastructure and services for data storage, processing, and advanced analytics.

Consider a scenario in the healthcare industry. A hospital uses Power BI to track patient data and operational metrics. Azure's capabilities, including Azure Data Lake Storage and Azure Machine Learning, enable the hospital to process vast amounts of patient data, identify patterns, and predict patient outcomes. The results are visualized in Power BI, giving healthcare providers the insights needed to make informed decisions in real-time.

The synergy of these two technologies creates a data ecosystem where data is collected, processed, and presented seamlessly. You'll learn how this integration works and how to harness it effectively as you progress through this book.

1.2 Who Should Read This Book

Data Analysts and Business Intelligence Professionals

Data analysts and business intelligence professionals play a pivotal role in transforming raw data into actionable insights. This book is tailor-made for individuals in these roles, whether you're just starting or looking to expand your knowledge.

Imagine you're a data analyst working for a retail company. Your task is to uncover sales trends and customer behaviors. Power BI and Azure offer you the ability to ingest large volumes of sales and customer data, perform advanced analytics, and visualize the results. With Power BI's intuitive interface, you can create interactive dashboards that reveal vital insights, such as the impact of marketing campaigns on sales. This book will guide you through the process, from data ingestion to creating compelling visualizations, empowering you to make data-driven decisions.

Data Engineers and Developers

Data engineers and developers are responsible for building the infrastructure and applications that enable data analytics. Whether you're managing data pipelines or creating custom solutions, this book provides insights into integrating Power BI and Azure effectively.

For instance, consider a data engineer responsible for building a data pipeline for a manufacturing company. In this scenario, the engineer uses Azure Data Factory to ingest data from sensors on the factory floor. They then utilize Azure Data Lake Storage to store and manage this data efficiently. By integrating Power BI, the engineer creates real-time dashboards that track machine performance. This book will provide a comprehensive guide on building such data pipelines and integrating them with Power BI to provide valuable insights.

IT Managers and Decision-Makers

IT managers and decision-makers need a solid understanding of the potential of Power BI and Azure to make informed choices for their organizations.

Imagine you're an IT manager for a financial institution. Your organization is looking to enhance its analytics capabilities to detect fraudulent transactions. Azure's advanced analytics services, such as Azure Machine Learning, can build robust models to identify suspicious activities. Power BI can then visualize these insights, making it easier for your security team to respond swiftly. Understanding how these tools work together is essential for making strategic decisions.

1.3 Setting the Stage: Cloud Analytics and Scalable Solutions

The Benefits of Cloud-Based Analytics

Cloud-based analytics offers a multitude of advantages, making it a fundamental component in modern data-driven strategies. To appreciate its significance, let's delve into some specific benefits.

Imagine a global e-commerce company. During a major shopping event, their website experiences a sudden surge in traffic. In a traditional on-premises environment, managing this influx of data would be a daunting challenge. With cloud-based analytics, the company can seamlessly scale its resources to accommodate the surge, ensuring that every transaction is processed in real-time. The cloud's elasticity enables the company to pay only for the resources it uses, optimizing cost-effectiveness.

Another critical benefit is accessibility. Cloud analytics allows data to be accessed and analyzed from anywhere, promoting collaboration and real-time decision-making. Employees across the globe can log into their analytics platforms, such as Power BI, to gain insights that are critical for their roles. In the context of the e-commerce company, marketing teams can monitor campaign performance, and customer support teams can respond to inquiries promptly.

The Challenge of Scalability

Scalability is a formidable challenge for traditional on-premises solutions. When data volumes grow, so do the complexities of managing and processing that data. Here's where the cloud's inherent scalability comes into play.

Let's consider a manufacturing company with a rapidly expanding dataset. In the cloud, they can seamlessly scale their data storage and processing capabilities as the volume of data grows. Azure, as a cloud platform, provides the tools and resources to make this scaling efficient and cost-effective. This scalability ensures that the company's analytics solutions remain high-performing, even as data volume increases.

The cloud's ability to scale up or down in response to demand also addresses seasonal fluctuations. For example, a retail business experiences significantly higher data processing needs during holiday seasons. Azure's autoscaling capabilities enable the company to provision additional resources when required and scale down during quieter periods. This adaptability optimizes resource utilization and cost-effectiveness.

The Promise of Power BI and Azure Integration

The promise of integrating Power BI with Azure represents the culmination of cloud analytics and scalability benefits. This integration allows organizations to build comprehensive data analytics solutions that are both scalable and cost-effective.

Consider a scenario where a financial institution needs to monitor real-time transactions and detect anomalies. Azure's Stream Analytics can process these transactions in real-time, while Power BI visualizes the results. Security teams can instantly identify and respond to fraudulent activities. This integration combines the strengths of both tools to deliver a powerful solution.

As you progress through this book, you'll gain a deep understanding of how to harness the promise of Power BI and Azure integration to build scalable, cost-effective, and user-friendly data analytics solutions.

CHAPTER I
Azure Fundamentals

2.1 Understanding Microsoft Azure

An Overview of Microsoft's Cloud Platform

Microsoft Azure is a comprehensive cloud computing platform that offers a wide range of services for building, deploying, and managing applications through Microsoft-managed data centers. Azure provides an extensive set of tools and services that empower organizations to leverage the cloud for various purposes, from hosting websites and applications to data storage, analytics, and more. In this section, we will provide an in-depth overview of Microsoft Azure, its core concepts, and how to get started.

What is Microsoft Azure?

At its core, Microsoft Azure is a collection of cloud services, including computing, analytics, storage, and networking, offered over the internet. These services can be broadly categorized into three main types:

1. Infrastructure as a Service (IaaS): In this model, Azure provides virtualized computing resources over the internet. Users can create, manage, and run virtual machines, servers, and other infrastructure components without having to invest in and maintain physical hardware. It's like having your data center in the cloud.

2. Platform as a Service (PaaS): Azure offers a platform for developers to build, deploy, and manage applications without worrying about the underlying infrastructure. This allows developers to focus solely on their code and application logic. Common examples include Azure App Service for web apps and Azure Functions for serverless computing.

3. Software as a Service (SaaS): Azure provides a wide range of SaaS applications that are ready to use. These include Microsoft 365, Dynamics 365, and more. SaaS applications eliminate the need for users to install and maintain software, as everything is hosted and managed by Azure.

Azure Regions and Data Centers

Azure operates in data centers located around the world. These data centers are grouped into geographic regions to provide data residency and compliance options. Each region consists of multiple data centers equipped with redundant power, cooling, and networking to ensure high availability and reliability.

For instance, the "East US" region encompasses multiple data centers in the eastern United States. Azure customers can choose the region that best suits their needs, taking into account factors like data sovereignty, latency, and disaster recovery requirements.

Getting Started with Microsoft Azure

Now that we've covered the basics, let's discuss how to get started with Microsoft Azure:

1. Create an Azure Account: To begin, you'll need an Azure account. If you don't already have one, you can sign up on the Azure website. Azure often offers a free trial with a credit to explore its services without any initial cost.

2. Azure Portal: The Azure Portal is the web-based interface for managing your Azure resources. Once you've created an account, you can log in to the Azure Portal to access and manage your Azure services.

3. Azure Services: Azure provides a vast array of services, from virtual machines and databases to machine learning and IoT. You can use the Azure Portal to create and manage these services. For example, you can deploy a virtual machine by selecting the Virtual Machines service and following the step-by-step wizard.

4. Command-Line Interface (CLI): Azure also offers a command-line interface, the Azure CLI, which allows you to manage your resources from your terminal or command prompt. It's a powerful tool for automating tasks and managing resources programmatically.

5. Azure Documentation and Learning Resources: Azure offers extensive documentation, tutorials, and learning resources on its website. These resources provide in-depth guidance on using Azure services, including code examples and best practices.

Let's conclude this overview by emphasizing that Microsoft Azure is a versatile cloud platform that can be tailored to meet the specific needs of your organization. Whether you're a developer, IT professional, or business decision-maker, Azure provides the tools and services to build, deploy, and scale applications and solutions effectively.

In the next sub-section, we will dive deeper into the concept of Azure Regions and Data Centers. If you have any questions or need further clarification, feel free to ask.

Azure Regions and Data Centers

Azure's global reach is one of its defining features. It spans a vast network of data centers across the world, with each region providing a specific geographical presence. These regions are strategically distributed to accommodate data residency requirements, enhance availability, and minimize latency. For example, the "East US" region has data centers on the eastern coast of the United States.

Why Azure Regions Matter

1. Data Residency: Many industries have strict regulations regarding where data can be stored. Azure's regions allow organizations to choose a region that complies with their data residency requirements. For instance, a European company might opt for the "North Europe" region to ensure data is stored within the EU.

2. Availability and Redundancy: Azure regions are equipped with multiple data centers. This redundancy ensures that if one data center experiences an issue, services can seamlessly failover to another data center within the same region. This results in high availability and business continuity.

3. Latency Optimization: When data is stored in a region physically closer to the users, it reduces the latency in data access. Low latency is crucial for responsive applications. For instance, a gaming company might host game servers in regions close to their players to minimize lag.

Selecting an Azure Region

Here's a step-by-step guide on how to select and deploy resources in an Azure region:

1. Log into Azure Portal: Access the Azure Portal using your Azure account credentials.

2. Create a Resource: Click on the "+ Create a resource" button in the Azure Portal. This action opens a new resource creation wizard.

3. Choose a Resource: Select the type of resource you want to create, such as a virtual machine, a database, or a web app.

4. Select a Region: During the resource creation process, you'll be prompted to choose the Azure region where the resource will be deployed. You can use the drop-down menu to browse and select your preferred region.

5. Review and Create: Complete the resource creation wizard, providing any necessary configuration details, and review your choices.

6. Create the Resource: After confirming your choices, click the "Create" button to deploy the resource in the chosen Azure region.

Code Example - Selecting an Azure Region in Azure CLI:

```bash
# Log in to your Azure account (if not already logged in)
az login

# List available regions
az account list-locations

# Create a resource group in a specific region
az group create --name MyResourceGroup --location eastus
```

The example above demonstrates how you can use Azure CLI to select a specific region while creating a resource group. The `--location` flag allows you to specify the desired Azure region.

Selecting the right Azure region is essential for optimizing performance and compliance for your applications and services. Make sure to consider data residency, availability, and latency when making your decision.

Azure Resource Groups

Azure Resource Groups are an essential organizational construct in Microsoft Azure, designed to simplify the management and grouping of Azure resources. They serve as containers for related resources that belong to a single solution, application, or environment. In this section, we'll explore what Azure Resource Groups are, why they are important, and how to create and manage them.

What Are Azure Resource Groups?

Azure Resource Groups are logical containers for Azure resources. They are used to group related resources together for easier management, organization, and monitoring. Think of them as a way to organize and manage resources in a structured manner.

For example, if you're building a web application, your Azure Resource Group might contain resources like a web app, a database, a storage account, and a virtual network. This grouping allows you to manage, monitor, and secure these resources collectively as a single unit.

Why Azure Resource Groups Matter

Azure Resource Groups offer several key advantages:

1. Organized Management: Resource Groups help you organize and manage resources more efficiently. By grouping resources that belong to the same application or project, you can easily locate and work with them.

2. Resource Deletion: Deleting a Resource Group means deleting all resources within it. This simplifies resource cleanup when you no longer need a set of related resources.

3. Role-Based Access Control: Azure Resource Groups allow you to apply role-based access control (RBAC) to the group itself. You can grant specific permissions to users or applications at the group level, which then applies to all resources within the group.

Creating an Azure Resource Group

Here's a step-by-step guide on how to create an Azure Resource Group:

1. Log into Azure Portal: Access the Azure Portal using your Azure account credentials.

2. Create a Resource Group: Click on the "+ Create a resource" button in the Azure Portal. In the search bar, type "Resource Group" and select the "Resource Group" service.

3. Create the Resource Group: In the "Resource Group" creation wizard, provide a name for the Resource Group, select your desired subscription, and choose a region. Regions are optional, but specifying a region helps in resource organization. Click the "Review + create" button to proceed.

4. Review and Create: Review the settings and configurations for your Resource Group. Once you're satisfied, click the "Create" button.

Code Example - Creating an Azure Resource Group in Azure CLI:

```bash
# Log in to your Azure account (if not already logged in)
az login


# Create a resource group
az group create --name MyResourceGroup --location eastus
```

The example above demonstrates how you can use Azure CLI to create a new Azure Resource Group. The `--name` flag specifies the name of the Resource Group, and the `--location` flag sets the region for the Resource Group.

Managing Resources Within an Azure Resource Group

Once a Resource Group is created, you can add, modify, and delete resources within it using the Azure Portal, Azure CLI, or other Azure management tools. Resources can include virtual machines, databases, web apps, and more.

Azure Resource Groups make it easier to apply RBAC, monitor resource usage, and enforce security policies at a group level, enhancing the overall management of Azure resources.

2.2 Azure Services for Data and Analytics

Azure Data Services

Azure offers a rich ecosystem of data services designed to facilitate the storage, management, and processing of data. Azure Data Services provide the foundation for building robust data solutions, and in this section, we'll explore key data services, why they are essential, and how to work with them.

Azure Data Services Overview

Azure Data Services cover a wide range of data-related solutions, each catering to different aspects of data management and analysis. These services enable you to store and manage data efficiently, whether it's structured, semi-structured, or unstructured. They also offer options for data transformation, migration, and analytics.

Here are some core Azure Data Services:

1. Azure SQL Database: This is a fully managed relational database service in the cloud. It allows you to create, manage, and scale relational databases without worrying about the underlying infrastructure.

2. Azure Cosmos DB: A globally distributed, multi-model database service for building highly responsive and scalable applications. It supports various data models, including document, key-value, graph, and column-family.

3. Azure Data Lake Storage: A scalable and secure data lake that can store and analyze massive volumes of data. It's designed for big data analytics and supports a variety of data types.

4. Azure Blob Storage: A versatile object storage service for unstructured data. It's ideal for serving content, such as images, videos, and backups, and can be used in various data scenarios.

Why Azure Data Services Matter

Azure Data Services offer several advantages:

1. Scalability: Azure Data Services can scale vertically or horizontally based on your requirements. This scalability is vital when dealing with data growth or varying workloads.

2. Managed Services: Azure takes care of the infrastructure management, including updates, backups, and patching. This reduces the operational overhead for IT teams.

3. High Availability: Data services are designed for high availability and disaster recovery. Data is often replicated across multiple regions, ensuring data durability and business continuity.

4. Security: Azure provides robust security features to protect your data, including encryption at rest and in transit, identity and access management, and compliance certifications.

Working with Azure Data Services

Here's a general outline of how to work with Azure Data Services:

1. Create a Data Service: Depending on the data service you need, you can create it via the Azure Portal, Azure CLI, or other Azure management tools.

2. Set Up Data: Once the data service is created, you can start ingesting data. For example, with Azure SQL Database, you can create tables, and for Azure Data Lake Storage, you can upload data files.

3. Access and Query Data: Utilize the respective tools and languages to access and query your data. For Azure SQL Database, you can use SQL queries, and for Azure Cosmos DB, you can use APIs like SQL, Gremlin, or MongoDB.

Code Example - Creating an Azure SQL Database in Azure CLI:

```bash
# Log in to your Azure account (if not already logged in)
az login


# Create an Azure SQL Database
az sql db create --resource-group MyResourceGroup --server MyServer --name MySampleDB --service-objective S0
```

The code above demonstrates how to use Azure CLI to create an Azure SQL Database. It specifies the resource group, server, database name, and the service objective.

Conclusion

Azure Data Services are the cornerstone of effective data management and analysis in the cloud. They provide the necessary tools and infrastructure to store, process, and analyze data, making them essential for various data-driven applications and solutions.

Azure Analytics Services

Azure Analytics Services encompass a set of tools and services that facilitate data analysis, transformation, visualization, and insights. These services empower organizations to extract valuable information from their data, enabling data-driven decision-making. In this section, we'll dive into some key Azure Analytics Services, why they are significant, and how to work with them.

Azure Analytics Services Overview

Azure Analytics Services provide a comprehensive set of tools to process, analyze, and visualize data. They cater to various aspects of data analytics and offer solutions for different use cases. Here are a few prominent Azure Analytics Services:

1. Azure Databricks: A collaborative Apache Spark-based analytics platform for big data and machine learning. It provides an interactive workspace for data engineers, data scientists, and analysts.

2. Azure Synapse Analytics: A limitless analytics service that brings together big data and data warehousing into a unified platform. It allows you to analyze both structured and unstructured data at scale.

3. Azure Stream Analytics: A real-time data stream processing service. It enables the analysis of data from devices, sensors, applications, and other streaming sources to extract insights and trigger actions in real-time.

4. Power BI: While not exclusive to Azure, Power BI is a powerful data visualization and business intelligence tool that integrates seamlessly with Azure services. It allows you to create interactive reports and dashboards.

Why Azure Analytics Services Matter

Azure Analytics Services offer several advantages:

1. Real-time Insights: Services like Azure Stream Analytics allow you to process and gain insights from streaming data in real-time, making it valuable for IoT applications and real-time monitoring.

2. Scalability: These services can scale to handle large datasets and complex computations, ensuring that you can process data efficiently as your needs grow.

3. Integration: Azure Analytics Services seamlessly integrate with other Azure data services, enabling you to create end-to-end data solutions.

4. Collaboration: Services like Azure Databricks provide a collaborative environment where data engineers, data scientists, and analysts can work together to solve data-related challenges.

Working with Azure Analytics Services

Here's a general outline of how to work with Azure Analytics Services:

1. Select the Right Service: Choose the Azure Analytics Service that best fits your analytics needs. Depending on your use case, you may opt for real-time data processing with Azure Stream Analytics or big data analytics with Azure Databricks.

2. Ingest Data: Ingest the data you want to analyze into the chosen service. This may involve setting up data pipelines or connecting to data sources.

3. Data Transformation: Transform the data as needed. This can include cleaning, aggregating, and structuring data for analysis.

4. Analysis and Visualization: Perform data analysis using tools and languages specific to the service. For example, Azure Databricks uses Apache Spark for data processing, while Power BI offers a visual interface for report creation.

Code Example - Setting Up Azure Stream Analytics Job in Azure Portal:

Setting up an Azure Stream Analytics job primarily involves defining inputs, queries, and outputs. Here's an example of how you can set up a Stream Analytics job in the Azure Portal:

1. In the Azure Portal, create a Stream Analytics job.

2. Configure your input, such as an Azure Event Hub or IoT Hub, where the streaming data originates.

3. Define a query to transform and analyze the data as it flows through the job.

4. Configure the output, which can be various Azure services like Azure SQL Database, Azure Cosmos DB, or Azure Blob Storage.

Conclusion

Azure Analytics Services are essential components for organizations looking to harness the power of data. Whether you need real-time insights, big data analytics, or interactive data visualization, Azure offers a variety of services to meet your analytics requirements.

Azure Integration Services

Azure Integration Services encompass a set of tools and services that facilitate the integration of data, applications, and services within Azure and beyond. These services play a critical role in connecting and orchestrating various components of a system. In this section, we'll delve into some key Azure Integration Services, why they are significant, and how to work with them.

Azure Integration Services Overview

Azure Integration Services offer capabilities for connecting applications, services, and data across various environments. They provide solutions for data integration, messaging, API management, and workflow automation. Here are a few essential Azure Integration Services:

1. Azure Logic Apps: A cloud-based service that allows you to create and run workflows that integrate with various Azure and non-Azure services. Logic Apps make it easy to automate business processes.

2. Azure Service Bus: A messaging service for connecting applications or services. It supports both message queues and publish-subscribe topics, enabling reliable message-based communication.

3. Azure API Management: A full-featured API gateway that enables you to create, publish, secure, and analyze APIs. It's crucial for exposing and managing APIs within your organization.

4. Azure Data Factory: A data integration service for creating, scheduling, and orchestrating data pipelines. It allows you to move data from various sources to destinations for analytics and reporting.

Why Azure Integration Services Matter

Azure Integration Services offer several advantages:

1. Connectivity: They enable seamless connectivity between various services and applications, both in the cloud and on-premises.

2. Orchestration: Integration Services allow you to create complex workflows and orchestrations, automating business processes and data movement.

3. Scalability: These services can scale to handle increased workloads, ensuring that your integration solutions can grow with your needs.

4. Monitoring and Analytics: Integration Services provide monitoring and analytics capabilities, allowing you to gain insights into the health and performance of your integrations.

Working with Azure Integration Services

Here's a general outline of how to work with Azure Integration Services:

1. Select the Right Service: Choose the Azure Integration Service that aligns with your integration needs. For example, use Azure Logic Apps for workflow automation or Azure Data Factory for data integration.

2. Create the Integration: Using the chosen service, create and configure the integration by defining triggers, actions, connections, and data mappings.

3. Monitoring and Troubleshooting: Utilize the monitoring and analytics features provided by the service to track the health and performance of your integrations. This can include tracking successful runs, detecting failures, and setting up alerts.

Code Example - Creating a Simple Logic App Workflow:

Logic Apps use a visual designer to create workflows, but they can also be exported as code for more advanced scenarios. Here's an example of a simple Logic App workflow:

1. Create a Logic App in the Azure Portal.

2. Define a trigger, such as "When a new email arrives."

3. Add actions like "Create a file" in OneDrive or "Send an email."

4. Configure the actions with details like the file name or email recipient.

5. Save and run the Logic App. It will automatically trigger when a new email arrives and execute the defined actions.

Conclusion

Azure Integration Services are fundamental for enabling seamless communication, data integration, and workflow automation in your organization's technology stack. Whether you need to connect applications, manage APIs, or automate business processes, Azure provides the necessary tools and services to meet your integration requirements.

2.3 Azure Resource Management

Managing Azure Resources with the Azure Portal

The Azure Portal is a web-based, unified interface that allows you to manage and interact with your Azure resources efficiently. It provides an intuitive and user-friendly way to create, configure, and monitor your Azure resources. In this section, we will explore how to manage Azure resources using the Azure Portal, including creating, modifying, and monitoring resources.

Overview of Managing Azure Resources with the Azure Portal

The Azure Portal is the primary interface for managing Azure resources, making it the go-to choice for many users. Here are some key actions you can perform using the Azure Portal:

1. Resource Creation: You can create various types of Azure resources, such as virtual machines, databases, storage accounts, and more, through a guided process.

2. Resource Configuration: After creating a resource, you can configure its settings, adjust performance parameters, and customize it to meet your specific needs.

3. Monitoring: The Azure Portal provides real-time insights into your resources, including performance metrics, health status, and usage statistics. You can set up alerts for resource monitoring.

4. Resource Management: The Azure Portal allows you to manage resources by starting, stopping, restarting, or deleting them. You can also organize resources into resource groups.

How to Manage Azure Resources with the Azure Portal

Let's take a step-by-step look at how to manage Azure resources using the Azure Portal:

1. Log in to Azure Portal: Go to the [Azure Portal](https://portal.azure.com/) and log in with your Azure account credentials.

2. Navigate to Resources: On the left-hand menu, you will find various options like "Home," "Resource groups," "Create a resource," and more. Click on "Resource groups" to see a list of your existing resource groups.

3. Create a Resource: To create a new resource, click on "Create a resource" in the left menu or from within a specific resource group. Follow the guided steps to select the resource type and configure its settings.

4. Resource Configuration: After creating a resource, click on the resource name within a resource group. Here, you can configure settings, adjust performance parameters, and modify the resource to suit your requirements.

5. Monitoring and Alerts: From the resource's overview page, you can access monitoring and alerts. Configure metrics and set up alerts to be notified of resource performance or health issues.

Example: Creating an Azure Virtual Machine in the Azure Portal

Here's an example of how to create an Azure Virtual Machine (VM) using the Azure Portal:

1. Log in to the Azure Portal.

2. Click "Create a resource" in the left menu.

3. Search for "Virtual Machine" and select the "Windows Virtual Machine" or "Linux Virtual Machine" option, depending on your preference.

4. Follow the guided steps to configure the VM, including specifying the operating system, size, networking options, and more.

5. Review your settings, click "Review + create," and then click "Create" to create the VM.

The Azure Portal will guide you through the entire process, and you can monitor the VM's status and performance from the portal.

Conclusion

The Azure Portal is a powerful and user-friendly tool for managing Azure resources. It simplifies resource creation, configuration, and monitoring, making it an excellent choice for users of all levels of expertise. Whether you're creating virtual machines, databases, or other Azure resources, the portal provides a streamlined way to interact with the Azure platform.

Azure Resource Manager (ARM)

Azure Resource Manager, often abbreviated as ARM, is the management framework for Azure that enables you to deploy, manage, and organize Azure resources efficiently. It offers a consistent and unified way to work with Azure resources, allowing you to describe your infrastructure as code, automate resource provisioning, and manage resources as a group.

Overview of Azure Resource Manager (ARM)

Azure Resource Manager provides several key capabilities and features:

1. Resource Group: ARM allows you to organize related resources into resource groups. This simplifies resource management, as you can treat the entire resource group as a single entity.

2. Resource Deployment Templates: You can use Azure Resource Manager templates to define your infrastructure as code. These templates are written in JSON and describe the resources and their configurations. This approach ensures consistent and repeatable deployments.

3. Role-Based Access Control (RBAC): ARM offers granular access control through RBAC. This allows you to define who can access, modify, or delete resources, ensuring security and compliance.

4. Resource Tagging: You can tag resources to categorize and label them. This is helpful for cost management, resource tracking, and organization.

5. Resource Dependencies: ARM allows you to define dependencies between resources. For example, a virtual machine may depend on a virtual network. ARM ensures resources are provisioned in the correct order.

How to Work with Azure Resource Manager (ARM)

Here's an overview of how to work with Azure Resource Manager:

1. Resource Group Creation: Start by creating a resource group. A resource group is a logical container that holds related Azure resources. You can create resource groups through the Azure Portal, Azure CLI, Azure PowerShell, or ARM templates.

2. Resource Template: Define an ARM template, which is a JSON file describing the resources you want to create. This template includes resource types, names, properties, and dependencies.

3. Deployment: Use the Azure Portal, Azure CLI, or Azure PowerShell to deploy your template. The template is submitted, and ARM orchestrates the deployment, creating the specified resources in the resource group.

4. RBAC: Configure Role-Based Access Control (RBAC) to control who can manage, modify, or delete resources within the resource group.

5. Monitoring and Management: Monitor your resources and resource group from the Azure Portal. You can also manage resources collectively by performing actions on the entire resource group.

Example: Deploying a Virtual Machine Using an ARM Template

Here's an example of deploying an Azure Virtual Machine using an ARM template:

1. Create an ARM template (in JSON format) that defines the virtual machine's properties, such as its size, operating system, network configuration, and dependencies.

2. Deploy the ARM template using the Azure Portal, Azure CLI, or Azure PowerShell. The template specifies the virtual machine's configuration.

3. Azure Resource Manager orchestrates the deployment, creating the virtual machine and any associated resources.

4. You can monitor and manage the virtual machine and other related resources from the Azure Portal or using Azure management tools.

Conclusion

Azure Resource Manager (ARM) is a crucial component for efficiently managing Azure resources. It provides a structured and automated way to deploy, manage, and organize resources, ensuring consistency and repeatability in resource management. Whether you're creating a single virtual machine or an entire application stack, ARM simplifies the process and enhances resource management.

Azure PowerShell and Azure CLI

Azure PowerShell and Azure Command-Line Interface (Azure CLI) are powerful tools that allow you to manage and automate Azure resources using command-line interfaces. They provide flexibility and scalability for managing resources programmatically, which is especially useful for large-scale deployments and repetitive tasks.

Overview of Azure PowerShell and Azure CLI

1. Azure PowerShell:

  - Azure PowerShell is a module that extends Windows PowerShell with cmdlets specifically for managing Azure resources.

  - It provides seamless integration with Azure, allowing you to automate tasks, manage resources, and deploy solutions.

  - Azure PowerShell offers both Azure Service Management (ASM) cmdlets and Azure Resource Manager (ARM) cmdlets. ARM cmdlets are recommended for use with modern Azure deployments.

2. Azure CLI:

- Azure CLI is a cross-platform command-line tool that provides a consistent experience for managing Azure resources across different platforms (Windows, macOS, and Linux).

- It uses a simple and easy-to-learn syntax based on commands.

- Azure CLI is designed for use with Azure Resource Manager and is well-suited for working with ARM templates and modern Azure deployments.

How to Use Azure PowerShell and Azure CLI

Here's an overview of how to use Azure PowerShell and Azure CLI to manage Azure resources:

Azure PowerShell:

1. Installation:

- Install Azure PowerShell by running the following command in Windows PowerShell:

```powershell
Install-Module -Name Az
```

2. Authentication:

- Authenticate to your Azure subscription using the `Connect-AzAccount` cmdlet. You can sign in with your Azure credentials.

3. Resource Management:

- Use Azure PowerShell cmdlets to create, manage, and configure Azure resources. For example, you can create virtual machines, storage accounts, or web apps.

4. Scripting and Automation:

   - Azure PowerShell is ideal for scripting and automation. You can write scripts to perform complex tasks and automate resource provisioning.

Azure CLI:

1. Installation:

   - Install Azure CLI on your local machine by following the installation instructions for your specific platform.

2. Authentication:

   - Sign in to your Azure subscription using the `az login` command. This will open a browser window for authentication.

3. Resource Management:

   - Use Azure CLI commands to interact with Azure resources. For instance, you can create virtual networks, manage databases, or deploy web apps.

4. Scripting and Automation:

   - Azure CLI is suitable for scripting and automation. You can write bash scripts or batch files to automate resource management tasks.

Example: Using Azure CLI to Create an Azure Virtual Machine:

```bash
# Sign in to your Azure account
```

```
az login


# Create a resource group

az group create --name MyResourceGroup --location eastus


# Create a virtual machine

az vm create --resource-group MyResourceGroup --name MyVM --image UbuntuLTS --admin-username azureuser --admin-password MyPassword
```


Conclusion

Azure PowerShell and Azure CLI are essential tools for managing Azure resources using command-line interfaces. They provide flexibility, automation capabilities, and a consistent experience for Azure resource management across platforms. Whether you need to create and configure resources, automate tasks, or work with ARM templates, these tools are indispensable for Azure administrators and developers.

CHAPTER II
Power BI Basics

3.1 A Primer on Power BI

The Power BI Ecosystem

Power BI is a comprehensive business intelligence and data visualization tool developed by Microsoft. It offers a wide array of features and components that together form the Power BI ecosystem, which empowers users to gather, analyze, and visualize data effectively.

Understanding the Power BI Ecosystem

The Power BI ecosystem consists of several key components:

1. Power BI Desktop:

  - Power BI Desktop is a Windows application that allows users to create interactive reports and data models. It provides a powerful and intuitive interface for data transformation, visualization, and report design.

  - To get started with Power BI Desktop, follow these steps:

  - **Installation:** Download and install Power BI Desktop from the [Power BI website](https://powerbi.microsoft.com/desktop).

  - **Data Import:** Connect to various data sources, import data, and transform it as needed.

  - **Data Modeling:** Create relationships between tables, define measures, and enhance data for reporting.

- **Report Building:** Design interactive reports and dashboards with charts, tables, visuals, and filters.

- **Publishing:** Publish the created reports to the Power BI Service or Power BI Report Server.

2. Power BI Service:

- Power BI Service is a cloud-based platform for sharing, collaborating, and distributing Power BI reports. It allows users to access reports from anywhere with an internet connection.

- To use Power BI Service:

- **Subscription:** Sign up for a Power BI Pro or Power BI Premium subscription.

- **Publishing Reports:** Upload reports created in Power BI Desktop to the Power BI Service.

- **Sharing:** Share reports and dashboards with colleagues, clients, or stakeholders.

- **Collaboration:** Collaborate with team members in real-time by creating and editing reports together.

- **Data Refresh:** Schedule data refresh to keep reports up to date.

3. Power BI Mobile:

- Power BI Mobile is a mobile application available on various platforms (iOS, Android, Windows). It enables users to access and interact with Power BI reports on their mobile devices.

- To use Power BI Mobile:

- **Installation:** Download the Power BI Mobile app from your device's app store.

- **Sign In:** Sign in with your Power BI account to access your reports and dashboards.

- **Interactivity:** View and interact with reports, explore data, and share insights with colleagues on the go.

Example: Creating a Simple Power BI Report

Let's walk through a basic example of creating a Power BI report using Power BI Desktop:

1. Installation: Download and install Power BI Desktop.

2. Data Import: Launch Power BI Desktop, click on "Get Data," and connect to a data source (e.g., Excel, SQL Server, or an online service).

3. Data Transformation: Transform and clean the imported data using the Power Query Editor. You can filter, transform, or pivot data as needed.

4. Data Modeling: Define relationships between tables if working with multiple data sources. Create calculated columns and measures for data analysis.

5. Report Building: Design your report by adding visuals like charts, tables, and slicers to the report canvas. Arrange visuals to create an interactive dashboard.

6. Publishing: Save the report, and then publish it to the Power BI Service to share with others.

Conclusion

The Power BI ecosystem, consisting of Power BI Desktop, Power BI Service, and Power BI Mobile, offers a complete solution for data analysis and reporting. Users can create, share, and access reports from various devices and collaborate seamlessly. Understanding these components is essential for harnessing the full potential of Power BI for your data visualization and business intelligence needs.

Licensing and Pricing

Understanding the licensing and pricing model of Power BI is crucial for organizations and individuals looking to adopt this business intelligence and data visualization tool. Power BI offers various licensing options, each with its own features and pricing structure.

Licensing Options

1. Power BI Desktop:

- Power BI Desktop is a free, standalone application for report authoring. It allows you to create reports and dashboards without any licensing cost.

- It's ideal for individual users and analysts who need to build reports for personal use or share them with others.

2. Power BI Pro:

- Power BI Pro is a subscription-based service that costs $9.99 per user per month.

- With Power BI Pro, users can publish reports to the Power BI Service, collaborate with other users, share dashboards, and schedule data refresh.

- Report consumers, even those without a Power BI Pro license, can view shared reports and dashboards.

3. Power BI Premium:

- Power BI Premium is designed for organizations with a large number of users or dedicated capacity needs. Pricing varies based on the capacity size.

- It provides dedicated cloud capacity, allowing users to share reports with Free license users.

- Premium also offers features like AI capabilities, paginated reports, and enhanced dataflows.

4. Power BI Embedded:

- Power BI Embedded is intended for developers and ISVs (Independent Software Vendors) who want to embed Power BI reports and dashboards into custom applications.

- The pricing model is based on the number of rendered reports and is more complex, with different tiers and rates.

Pricing Considerations

When choosing a Power BI licensing option, consider the following factors:

1. User Needs: Evaluate the needs of your users. If you have a small team of authors and a larger number of consumers, Power BI Pro may be sufficient. For organizations with extensive collaboration and sharing requirements, Power BI Premium might be more cost-effective.

2. Scale: As your organization grows, you may need to scale up your Power BI licensing. Power BI Premium offers scalability, while Power BI Embedded is suitable for embedding reports in applications.

3. Total Cost of Ownership (TCO): Consider the overall TCO, which includes licensing, infrastructure costs, and maintenance. Power BI Premium might be more cost-effective for large user bases.

4. Data Security and Compliance: Ensure that your chosen licensing option aligns with your organization's data security and compliance requirements.

Example: Choosing the Right Power BI Licensing

Imagine you are the IT manager for a medium-sized company with 50 employees who need access to Power BI reports. Twenty of these employees will be report authors, and the remaining 30 will be consumers. In this case:

- Power BI Pro is suitable for your report authors since they need to create and publish reports.

- For the 30 consumers, you can choose between Power BI Pro and Power BI Premium. Power BI Pro may be more cost-effective, but Power BI Premium offers more scalability and features.

Conclusion

Understanding Power BI's licensing and pricing options is essential for making informed decisions about which license to choose. Whether you're an individual analyst or managing an organization's BI needs, selecting the right licensing option ensures that you have access to the features and capabilities required to meet your business intelligence and reporting goals.

Power BI Desktop vs. Power BI Service

Power BI provides two main ways to create, manage, and interact with your reports and dashboards: Power BI Desktop and Power BI Service. Understanding the differences and use cases for each is essential for effective data analysis and reporting.

Power BI Desktop

Power BI Desktop is a Windows application that is primarily used for authoring and creating reports. Here are some key characteristics of Power BI Desktop:

1. Report Creation: Power BI Desktop is the go-to tool for designing and building reports from scratch. It allows you to import data, create data models, design visuals, and create interactive dashboards.

2. Data Modeling: You can use Power Query to transform, clean, and shape your data. Power BI Desktop supports advanced data modeling techniques, such as defining relationships, creating calculated columns, and writing complex DAX (Data Analysis Expressions) formulas.

3. Report Authoring: You have full control over report design, including choosing visualizations, customizing colors and themes, and adding interactivity using slicers and filters.

4. Local Development: Power BI Desktop runs on your local machine, which means you can work on reports without an internet connection. It's suitable for offline report creation and development.

5. File-Based: Reports created in Power BI Desktop are saved as .pbix files, which can be shared and opened by other Power BI Desktop users.

Power BI Service

Power BI Service, on the other hand, is a cloud-based platform for sharing, collaborating, and consuming reports. Here's what you need to know about Power BI Service:

1. Report Sharing: Power BI Service allows you to publish and share reports created in Power BI Desktop with a broader audience. You can invite others to view and collaborate on reports, even if they don't have Power BI Desktop.

2. Accessibility: Reports hosted on Power BI Service are accessible from any device with an internet connection. Users can access reports on the web, mobile apps, and embedded in applications.

3. Collaboration: Power BI Service supports real-time collaboration, enabling multiple users to work on reports simultaneously. It also provides a commenting feature for discussions.

4. Data Refresh: Scheduling data refresh is a feature of Power BI Service, ensuring that reports are always up to date with the latest data from the source.

5. Sharing and Embedding: You can share reports externally with clients or partners and even embed them in websites or applications.

Choosing Between Power BI Desktop and Power BI Service

The choice between Power BI Desktop and Power BI Service depends on your role and specific needs:

- **Power BI Desktop** is ideal for report authors and analysts who need to create complex reports, design visuals, and perform advanced data modeling on their local machines. It is the starting point for creating reports.

- **Power BI Service** is for sharing, collaboration, and consuming reports. It is suitable for report consumers, stakeholders, and teams that need to access and interact with reports online. It enhances accessibility and collaboration features.

Example: Workflow from Power BI Desktop to Power BI Service

1. A data analyst uses Power BI Desktop to create a comprehensive sales report, including custom visuals and calculated measures.

2. The analyst publishes the report to Power BI Service.

3. Sales managers access the report on Power BI Service, apply filters, and drill down into the data to make business decisions.

4. The data analyst can schedule regular data refreshes in Power BI Service to keep the report up to date.

Conclusion

Power BI Desktop and Power BI Service complement each other in the Power BI ecosystem. While Power BI Desktop is used for report authoring and advanced data modeling, Power BI Service is designed for sharing, collaboration, accessibility, and data refresh. Understanding how to leverage both tools is essential for effective data analysis and reporting.

3.2 Power BI Service vs. Power BI Desktop

Authoring Reports and Dashboards in Power BI Desktop

Power BI Desktop is a powerful tool for creating detailed and interactive reports and dashboards. In this section, we will explore how to author reports and dashboards in Power BI Desktop, step by step.

Step 1: Launch Power BI Desktop

To get started, open Power BI Desktop on your computer. If you haven't already installed it, you can download it from the official Power BI website.

Step 2: Create a New Report

- When Power BI Desktop launches, you'll see a blank canvas. To start a new report, go to the "File" menu and select "New" or simply press Ctrl + N.

- You can also open an existing report by selecting "Open" and navigating to the report's .pbix file.

Step 3: Connect to Data

- To populate your report with data, you need to connect to data sources. Click on "Get Data" in the Home tab.

- Power BI Desktop supports a wide range of data sources, including databases, files, online services, and more. Select your data source, and follow the prompts to establish a connection.

Step 4: Transform and Shape Data

- Once you've connected to your data, you can use the Power Query Editor to transform and shape it. This is where you clean, filter, and structure your data to fit your reporting needs.

- The Power Query Editor provides a user-friendly interface for data transformations. You can remove duplicates, merge tables, create calculated columns, and perform other data operations.

Step 5: Build Visualizations

- With your data ready, it's time to create visualizations. In the "Visualizations" pane on the right, you'll find various chart types like bar charts, line charts, pie charts, and more.

- Simply drag and drop fields from your data onto the chart elements to create visuals. For example, you can drag a "Product Name" field to the "Axis" area and a "Sales Amount" field to the "Values" area to create a bar chart.

Step 6: Customize Visuals

- Power BI Desktop allows you to customize your visuals extensively. You can change colors, fonts, titles, and other formatting options to match your report's design.

- Use the "Format" and "Visualizations" panes to access customization options for individual visuals.

Step 7: Create Dashboards

- Dashboards are a collection of visuals and reports that provide a consolidated view of your data. You can create dashboards by clicking the "Create Dashboard" button in the left navigation pane.

- Add visuals and reports to the dashboard, arrange them, and customize the layout.

Step 8: Publish to Power BI Service

- To share your report with others, you need to publish it to Power BI Service. Click the "Publish" button in the "Home" tab.

- You'll be prompted to sign in to your Power BI account and select the workspace where you want to publish the report.

Step 9: Share and Collaborate

- In Power BI Service, you can share the report with specific users or groups. You can also set up automatic data refresh schedules and manage report access.

- Collaborate with colleagues by leaving comments, and take advantage of the collaboration features within Power BI Service.

Conclusion

Power BI Desktop is a comprehensive tool for report authoring. By following these steps, you can create, design, and customize interactive reports and dashboards that effectively communicate your data insights. Once your report is ready, you can publish it to Power BI Service to share it with a broader audience and collaborate seamlessly.

Publishing and Sharing Reports via Power BI Service

Once you've created and designed your reports and dashboards in Power BI Desktop, the next step is to publish and share them via Power BI Service. Here's how to do it, step by step:

Step 1: Save Your Report in Power BI Desktop

- Before you can publish your report, ensure that you've saved it in Power BI Desktop. Go to the "File" menu and select "Save" or "Save As" if you want to create a new file.

Step 2: Publish to Power BI Service

- To publish your report, click on the "Publish" button in the "Home" tab of Power BI Desktop.

- You'll be prompted to sign in to your Power BI account if you haven't already. Enter your credentials.

Step 3: Choose a Destination Workspace

- After signing in, you need to choose the destination workspace where you want to publish the report. Workspaces are containers for your reports and dashboards in Power BI Service.

- Select an existing workspace or create a new one, then click "Select."

Step 4: Configure Settings (Optional)

- You can configure settings for the report before publishing. This includes options like specifying the data source credentials, configuring automatic data refresh schedules, and setting up dataflows.

- Adjust these settings as needed.

Step 5: Publish the Report

- Click the "Publish" button to initiate the publishing process. Power BI Desktop will upload your report and its associated data to Power BI Service.

- Once the process is complete, you'll receive a confirmation message.

Step 6: Access Your Report in Power BI Service

- Open a web browser and navigate to Power BI Service (https://app.powerbi.com).

- Sign in to your Power BI account if you're not already logged in.

Step 7: Find Your Report in the Workspace

- In Power BI Service, navigate to the workspace where you published the report. You'll find your report listed among the items in that workspace.

Step 8: Interact with the Report

- Click on the report to open and interact with it in Power BI Service. You can apply filters, explore data, and create new visuals.

- Use the "File" menu to perform actions like exporting the report or creating a PDF snapshot.

Step 9: Share the Report

- To share your report, click the "Share" button in Power BI Service. You can share it with specific users, security groups, or with anyone who has the link.

- Configure permissions and set whether recipients can edit the report or view it only.

Step 10: Collaborate and Leave Comments

- Take advantage of the collaborative features in Power BI Service. You can leave comments on visuals and reports, which is especially useful for discussions and collaboration with colleagues.

- Use the commenting feature to provide context and insights.

Step 11: Data Refresh Scheduling

- In Power BI Service, you can set up data refresh schedules to keep your report up to date with the latest data from the source. This ensures that your audience always has access to current information.

Step 12: Embedded Reporting (Optional)

- If you want to embed your report in a website or application, you can use Power BI Embedded. This allows you to integrate your report in your custom applications.

Conclusion

Publishing and sharing reports via Power BI Service is essential for making your data insights accessible to a wider audience. You can easily share and collaborate with colleagues, partners, and clients, ensuring that everyone is on the same page when it comes to data analysis and reporting.

Collaborative Features of Power BI Service

Power BI Service offers a range of collaborative features that enable teams to work together, discuss insights, and make data-driven decisions. Here's a detailed guide on how to use these collaborative features effectively:

1. Sharing Reports and Dashboards

- In Power BI Service, you can share your reports and dashboards with colleagues and stakeholders. To do this, open the report or dashboard you want to share and click the "Share" button.

- Specify the recipients' email addresses or names, and choose their permissions: "Can view" or "Can edit." You can also create a shareable link that allows anyone with the link to access the report.

2. Collaborative Editing

- Collaborative editing allows multiple users to work on a report or dashboard simultaneously. When multiple people are editing the same report, you'll see their avatars in the top-right corner.

- Users can work on different parts of the report simultaneously. Changes are synchronized in real-time.

3. Comments and Discussions

- You can leave comments on visuals and reports in Power BI Service to discuss insights, ask questions, or provide additional context.

- To leave a comment, select a visual or a specific point in a visual, and click the comment icon. Type your comment and tag colleagues to notify them.

4. Notifications

- Stay informed about changes and discussions by using notifications. You'll receive notifications for comments, report changes, and shares.

- Notifications are accessible through the bell icon in the top-right corner of the Power BI Service interface.

5. Dashboard Sharing and Collaboration

- Collaborate on dashboards by sharing them with other users. Dashboards provide a consolidated view of data, making it easy for teams to focus on key insights.

- Share a dashboard with colleagues and set the permissions for viewing or editing. Collaborators can add their own visuals to the dashboard.

6. Publish to Web (Public Sharing)

- Power BI allows you to create public links (via "Publish to web") that can be embedded in websites, blogs, and social media. This is an option to share your insights with a broader audience.

- Use caution when using "Publish to web" for public sharing, as data may become accessible to anyone with the link.

7. Exporting Reports

- You can export reports to PDF, PowerPoint, or Excel formats, making it easy to share reports with people who don't have access to Power BI Service.

- The exported reports retain their interactivity, allowing viewers to explore the data.

8. Automatic Data Refresh and Scheduling

- Keep your reports up to date with automatic data refresh. You can set refresh schedules to ensure that the data in your reports is always current.

- Automatic refresh is particularly important for collaborative reports used by multiple users.

9. Power BI Mobile App

- Collaborate on the go using the Power BI mobile app. The app allows you to access your reports and dashboards, leave comments, and stay updated with notifications, even when you're away from your desk.

10. Usage Metrics

- Use usage metrics to track how your reports and dashboards are being used. This feature provides insights into who's viewing your content and how often.

- Understanding usage metrics can help tailor your content to your audience's needs.

Conclusion

Collaborative features in Power BI Service make it a valuable tool for teams to work together, discuss data insights, and make data-driven decisions. Whether you're sharing reports, collaborating in real-time, or leaving comments, these features enable effective teamwork and communication around data.

This concludes the exploration of "3.2 Power BI Service vs. Power BI Desktop - Collaborative Features of Power BI Service." If you have any questions or need further clarification, please feel free to ask.

3.3 Designing an Effective Data Model

Power BI Free, Pro, and Premium Licenses

Power BI offers a range of licensing options to accommodate various business needs. Understanding these licenses is crucial for selecting the right one for your organization. Let's explore the key aspects of Power BI Free, Power BI Pro, and Power BI Premium licenses:

1. Power BI Free

- Power BI Free is the basic, no-cost version of Power BI. It's an excellent choice for individual users and small businesses looking to get started with data visualization and reporting.

- With Power BI Free, users can create reports and dashboards, connect to various data sources, and share their work with others.

- However, there are limitations, such as limited data capacity and the inability to share content with users who don't have Power BI accounts.

2. Power BI Pro

- Power BI Pro is a subscription-based license that provides additional features and capabilities. It is ideal for businesses that require collaboration and sharing within their teams.

- With Power BI Pro, users can collaborate on reports and dashboards, share content with a broader audience, and schedule data refreshes. This license is assigned to individual users, and it comes with a monthly fee.

- Power BI Pro allows sharing with users who don't have Power BI accounts by using secure sharing links.

3. Power BI Premium

- Power BI Premium is designed for enterprises and large organizations. It offers dedicated capacity for data processing and sharing.

- With Power BI Premium, you can publish and share reports with external stakeholders without requiring them to have a Power BI Pro license.

- This license also provides greater scalability, improved performance, and the ability to manage workspaces and content more effectively.

- Power BI Premium is available in two flavors: Premium Per Capacity (PPC) and Premium Per User (PPU). PPU allows individual users to access premium features, while PPC provides dedicated capacity for the organization.

Selecting the Right License for Your Organization

Choosing the right Power BI license for your organization depends on your specific needs and budget. Consider the following factors:

- **Number of Users:** Determine how many users in your organization need access to Power BI. Power BI Pro licenses are assigned per user, while Power BI Premium offers more flexibility for larger user bases.

- **Data Requirements:** Assess your data needs, including data storage and data refresh frequency. Larger datasets and frequent data updates may benefit from Power BI Premium's enhanced capacity.

- **Collaboration:** If collaboration and sharing are crucial, Power BI Pro is a cost-effective solution. Power BI Premium is ideal if you need to share reports with external partners and clients.

- **Budget:** Evaluate your budget and licensing costs. Power BI Free is an option for those with limited budgets, while Power BI Premium suits organizations with larger budgets.

- **Scalability:** If your organization is growing, consider scalability. Power BI Premium offers scalability, so you can accommodate new users and increased data requirements.

Understanding these license options will help you make an informed decision on which Power BI license is the best fit for your organization's data analytics and reporting needs.

Power BI Embedded for Developers

Power BI Embedded is a powerful choice for developers who want to integrate interactive reports and dashboards into their applications, websites, or products. It provides the flexibility to embed Power BI visuals seamlessly. Here's a detailed look at Power BI Embedded for Developers:

What is Power BI Embedded?

Power BI Embedded is an Azure service that allows developers to integrate Power BI reports and dashboards directly into custom applications. Instead of requiring users to have individual Power BI licenses, this service enables you to deliver a rich, interactive data experience to your application's users without them needing a Power BI account.

Key Features of Power BI Embedded:

1. **Embedding Capabilities:** Power BI Embedded provides APIs and SDKs that allow developers to embed Power BI reports and dashboards within applications or websites. This embedded content remains interactive, and users can interact with visuals, drill into data, and apply filters.

2. Customization: Developers have full control over the look and feel of the embedded reports, including branding and integration with the application's user interface.

3. Multi-Tenancy: Power BI Embedded supports multi-tenancy, making it suitable for applications serving multiple clients or customers with varying data and reporting needs.

4. Capacity-based Licensing: Power BI Embedded is billed based on the capacity (virtual cores) you allocate, making it cost-effective and scalable.

How to Use Power BI Embedded:

1. Provisioning a Workspace: Developers can set up a dedicated workspace in the Power BI service where reports and dashboards are created and published.

2. Embedding with APIs: Use the Power BI Embedded REST APIs or client libraries to programmatically generate embed tokens and embed codes for reports and dashboards. Embed tokens are time-limited and provide secure access to the embedded content.

3. Embedding in Your Application: Insert the embed code into your application, web page, or product. You have the flexibility to customize the appearance and interactions of the embedded content.

4. Authentication and Security: Implement secure authentication methods for your application and ensure that only authorized users can access the embedded Power BI content.

Use Cases for Power BI Embedded:

- **Software as a Service (SaaS) Applications:** Embed reports and dashboards in SaaS applications to offer data analytics to your customers.

- **Custom Portals:** Develop custom portals or data-driven websites that incorporate interactive Power BI visuals.

- **Internal Applications:** Enhance internal applications with data visualizations, performance dashboards, and business intelligence capabilities.

Choosing the Right Licensing Model for Your Organization:

When deciding on Power BI licensing, it's crucial to understand your application's requirements. If you need to embed reports for external users or customers, Power BI Embedded is the ideal choice. It provides flexibility, customization, and cost-effective pricing based on your capacity needs.

Power BI Embedded empowers developers to create data-rich applications that deliver insights and analytics to users seamlessly. By understanding its capabilities and how to integrate it into your applications, you can enhance the value of your software offerings.

Choosing the Right Licensing Model for Your Organization

Selecting the appropriate Power BI licensing model for your organization is crucial to ensure that you have the right set of features, capabilities, and pricing that align with your business needs. Power BI offers different licensing options, and making the right choice is essential. Here's a detailed guide to help you choose the right licensing model for your organization:

Power BI Licensing Options:

1. Power BI Free: This is the entry-level licensing option and provides basic features for creating reports and dashboards. It's suitable for individual users or small-scale usage.

2. Power BI Pro: Power BI Pro is a user-based license that offers more advanced features, such as collaboration, sharing, and publishing reports to the Power BI Service. It is ideal for small to medium-sized teams and organizations.

3. Power BI Premium: Power BI Premium provides dedicated cloud capacity and is designed for large-scale deployments and enterprises. It allows for content distribution to a broader audience without requiring each user to have a Power BI Pro license.

4. Power BI Premium Per User (PPU): This is a user-based license that offers the premium capabilities of Power BI Premium to individual users, without the need for a full organization-wide Premium subscription.

Factors to Consider When Choosing a License:

1. User Base: Consider the number of users who need access to Power BI. If you have a small team or individual users, Power BI Pro or Free may be sufficient. For larger teams or organizations, Premium or PPU may be more appropriate.

2. Feature Requirements: Evaluate the features your organization needs. Power BI Pro and Premium offer more advanced capabilities like collaboration, app workspaces, and advanced data sharing.

3. Content Distribution: Determine how you want to distribute reports and dashboards. If you need to share content with a broad audience, Power BI Premium or PPU is suitable. If sharing is limited to a few users, Pro licenses may be sufficient.

4. Cost Considerations: Compare the cost of different licensing models based on the number of users and required features. Keep in mind that Power BI Pro and Premium are subscription-based, while Free is free but with limited capabilities.

Making the Decision:

1. Assess Your Needs: Begin by assessing your organization's specific requirements, including the number of users, features needed, and content distribution.

2. Evaluate Costs: Calculate the costs associated with each licensing option to determine which aligns with your budget.

3. Consider Growth: Think about your organization's potential growth. Choose a licensing model that can scale with your needs.

4. Review User Feedback: Gather feedback from users who will be using Power BI to understand their preferences and requirements.

5. Consult with Power BI Experts: If you're uncertain about which license to choose, consider consulting with Power BI experts or Microsoft representatives who can provide guidance.

Remember that you can mix and match different licensing models within your organization to meet different user needs. It's essential to regularly evaluate your licensing to ensure it still aligns with your evolving requirements.

Choosing the right licensing model is a fundamental step in effectively leveraging Power BI's capabilities within your organization. By considering factors such as user base, feature requirements, cost, and future growth, you can make an informed decision that best suits your organization's needs.

CHAPTER III
Data Preparation in Azure

4.1 Azure Data Factory: Data Ingestion and ETL

Introduction to Azure Data Factory

Azure Data Factory (ADF) is a cloud-based data integration service provided by Microsoft Azure. It allows you to create, schedule, and manage data-driven workflows for orchestrating and automating data movement and data transformation. ADF is a fundamental component in Azure's data and analytics ecosystem, serving as a powerful tool for ingesting, preparing, and transforming data for analysis and reporting.

Key Features and Capabilities:

1. Data Integration: ADF enables you to connect to various data sources, whether they are on-premises or in the cloud. It supports a wide range of data stores, databases, and file formats.

2. Data Orchestration: With ADF, you can create data pipelines that orchestrate the flow of data from source to destination. You can define dependencies and scheduling for activities in your pipelines.

3. Data Transformation: ADF includes data transformation activities, making it easy to transform data using Azure HDInsight Hadoop, Spark, Data Lake Analytics, and more. It also allows data wrangling with Power Query.

4. Monitoring and Management: ADF provides monitoring and management capabilities, allowing you to monitor the health and performance of your data pipelines. You can set up alerts, track activity runs, and manage triggers.

5. Security: ADF offers security features such as integration with Azure Active Directory for authentication and role-based access control (RBAC) for authorization.

Use Cases:

1. Data Migration: ADF can be used for moving data from on-premises systems to Azure, or between different Azure data stores.

2. Data Warehousing: ADF helps in populating and managing data warehouses, such as Azure SQL Data Warehouse, with data from various sources.

3. Data Transformation: You can perform data transformations and data wrangling tasks to prepare data for analytics and reporting.

4. Real-time Data Ingestion: ADF supports real-time data ingestion for streaming data, making it suitable for use cases involving IoT and real-time analytics.

Getting Started with Azure Data Factory:

1. Creating a Data Factory: Begin by creating an Azure Data Factory in the Azure portal. You can choose your region, resource group, and other settings.

2. Linked Services: Linked services are connections to your data stores and compute services. You'll need to set up linked services to connect to your data sources and destinations.

3. Datasets: Datasets represent your data structures. Define datasets for your source and target data stores. A dataset can be a table, a file, or a folder.

4. Pipelines: Pipelines are the heart of ADF. Create pipelines to define the activities and data flow in your data integration process.

5. Activities: Within pipelines, you define activities that perform actions like data movement or data transformation. There are various built-in activities to choose from.

6. Triggers: Set up triggers to schedule when your pipelines run. You can also create event-based triggers.

7. Monitoring: Use the monitoring and management features of ADF to track the execution and health of your data pipelines.

Example Scenario:

Suppose you have data stored in an on-premises SQL Server database, and you want to move this data to an Azure SQL Data Warehouse for analytical purposes. You can create an Azure Data Factory that connects to the on-premises database, extracts the data, and loads it into the Azure SQL Data Warehouse. You can schedule this pipeline to run at regular intervals to keep the data warehouse up to date.

By providing a unified platform for data integration and transformation, Azure Data Factory simplifies the task of managing your data workflows in a scalable and efficient manner.

Data Ingestion from On-Premises and Cloud Sources

One of the core capabilities of Azure Data Factory (ADF) is data ingestion, which involves extracting data from various sources, whether they are located on-premises or in the cloud. ADF provides a robust set of tools and connectors to help you efficiently collect and transfer data into your data pipelines for further processing.

Key Concepts:

1. Linked Services: Linked services act as connection strings that enable ADF to communicate with different data sources. You need to define linked services for each data source you want to ingest data from.

2. Data Movement Activities: ADF offers a range of data movement activities that facilitate data transfer between your source and destination. Some of the commonly used activities include:

  - **Copy Data Activity:** This activity is used for copying data from a source to a destination. It supports a wide variety of source and destination data stores.

  - **Data Flow Activity:** You can use this activity to perform data transformations and aggregations as part of the ingestion process. It's especially useful when the data needs to be transformed during ingestion.

Ingesting Data from Different Sources:

1. On-Premises Sources: ADF provides the Azure Data Factory Self-Hosted Integration Runtime, which acts as a bridge between your on-premises data sources and the Azure cloud. You can install the Integration Runtime on your on-premises data servers, allowing ADF to interact with them securely. Common on-premises sources include:

  - On-premises databases (e.g., SQL Server, Oracle)

  - On-premises file systems

- On-premises applications and logs

2. Cloud Sources: ADF seamlessly integrates with various cloud-based data sources, enabling you to ingest data from sources like:

- Azure Blob Storage

- Azure SQL Database

- Azure Data Lake Storage

- Azure Cosmos DB

- Various SaaS applications (e.g., Salesforce, Dynamics 365)

Steps to Perform Data Ingestion:

1. Define Linked Services: First, create linked services that establish connections to your source and destination data stores. These linked services contain connection information such as server details, authentication credentials, and other necessary parameters.

2. Create Datasets: Define datasets that represent your data structures. Datasets specify the format and location of your source data and destination data.

3. Build Pipelines: Design pipelines within ADF to orchestrate data ingestion workflows. In the pipeline, add data movement activities like "Copy Data" or "Data Flow" to specify what data to move and where to move it.

4. Set Up Triggers: Schedule your data pipelines to run at specific intervals or in response to events. ADF supports various trigger options for automation.

Example Scenario:

Let's say you want to ingest data from an on-premises SQL Server database into an Azure Data Lake Storage Gen2 account. Here are the steps to achieve this:

1. Create a Self-Hosted Integration Runtime on a server within your on-premises environment.

2. Define linked services for the SQL Server database (on-premises) and Azure Data Lake Storage (cloud-based).

3. Create datasets representing the tables in your SQL Server database and the target folder in Azure Data Lake Storage.

4. Build a data pipeline in ADF, adding a "Copy Data" activity that specifies the source and destination datasets.

5. Set up a trigger to run the pipeline at the desired schedule.

This will ensure that data is regularly ingested from the on-premises SQL Server database into Azure Data Lake Storage for further processing.

Data ingestion is a fundamental step in data preparation, as it ensures that your data is available in a centralized location for subsequent processing, transformation, and analysis.

Data Transformation with Azure Data Factory

Azure Data Factory (ADF) is a powerful cloud-based ETL (Extract, Transform, Load) service that allows you to perform data transformations as part of your data preparation process. Data transformation is crucial for converting raw data into a usable and insightful format. With ADF, you can design data transformation processes to clean, enrich, and reshape your data before it's loaded into a target data store.

Key Components for Data Transformation in ADF:

1. Data Flow: A data flow in ADF represents a sequence of data transformation steps. It can include various transformations like filtering, aggregating, joining, and pivoting data.

2. Activities: Activities are the individual tasks within a data flow that perform specific transformations. There are two primary types of activities for data transformation:

- **Mapping Data Flow Activity:** This activity is used to create a data transformation pipeline where you define transformations, source, and sink within a visual interface.

- **HDInsight Spark Job Activity:** If you need to perform complex transformations using Spark, you can use this activity.

3. Data Transformation Functions: ADF provides a wide range of transformation functions that you can apply to your data in data flows. These functions include data type conversions, data cleansing, and data manipulation functions.

Steps for Data Transformation with ADF:

1. Create a Data Flow: Start by creating a data flow in ADF using the Data Flow interface. You can use the drag-and-drop interface to design your data transformation process.

2. Add Data Transformation Activities: Inside your data flow, add activities to perform specific transformations. You can filter, aggregate, join, pivot, or perform custom transformations on your data.

3. Configure Data Sources and Sinks: Define your data sources (where the data originates) and sinks (where the transformed data will be stored). ADF supports various data sources, including Azure Blob Storage, Azure SQL Database, and more.

4. Apply Transformation Functions: Utilize built-in transformation functions to clean and enrich your data. These functions can be applied in your data flow activities.

5. Optimize Performance: ADF offers features to optimize the performance of your data transformations, such as partitioning, data skew handling, and parallelism settings.

Example Scenario:

Suppose you have a dataset with sales transactions, and you want to transform the data before loading it into a data warehouse. Here's how you can do it with Azure Data Factory:

1. Create a Data Flow in ADF and add a "Mapping Data Flow Activity."

2. Configure your source dataset, which contains raw sales data.

3. Add transformation steps within the data flow to clean the data, aggregate sales by product, and calculate total sales.

4. Define the sink dataset, which is your target data store, such as Azure SQL Data Warehouse.

5. Use data transformation functions to handle data type conversions and perform calculations.

6. Optimize the data flow for performance by configuring parallelism and data distribution.

Once the data flow is defined and scheduled, ADF will execute the data transformation steps at the specified intervals, ensuring that your transformed data is ready for analysis in your data warehouse.

Data transformation is a critical step in preparing data for analytics, as it ensures that data is accurate, consistent, and in the desired format for further analysis and reporting.

4.2 Azure Data Lake Storage: Storing and Managing Data

Understanding Azure Data Lake Storage

Azure Data Lake Storage is a scalable and secure data lake solution provided by Microsoft Azure for storing and managing vast amounts of data, including structured and unstructured data. It is designed to handle big data workloads and is integrated with other Azure services, making it an excellent choice for modern data analytics and data processing applications.

Key Features of Azure Data Lake Storage:

1. Scalability: Azure Data Lake Storage can handle massive amounts of data, from terabytes to petabytes, and can seamlessly scale based on your needs.

2. Storage Tiers: Data Lake Storage offers two storage tiers: hot and cold. Hot storage is optimized for frequently accessed data, while cold storage is cost-effective for less frequently accessed data.

3. Data Lake Storage Gen1 vs. Gen2: There are two generations of Azure Data Lake Storage:

  - **Data Lake Storage Gen1:** It was the initial version and offers a distributed file system with the capabilities to handle big data. However, it has some limitations in terms of performance and features.

  - **Data Lake Storage Gen2:** Gen2 is built on top of Azure Blob Storage and provides features like improved performance, security, and analytics capabilities. It offers a hierarchical file system that simplifies data management.

Core Concepts of Azure Data Lake Storage:

1. File System: Data in Azure Data Lake Storage is organized into a hierarchical file system, similar to a traditional file system. You can create directories, subdirectories, and store files within them.

2. Data Lake Storage REST API: You can interact with Data Lake Storage using REST APIs, which allows programmatic access to your data for tasks like uploading, downloading, and managing data.

3. Data Security: Azure Data Lake Storage provides advanced data security features, including Azure Active Directory integration, encryption at rest and in transit, and role-based access control (RBAC) for fine-grained access management.

Use Cases for Azure Data Lake Storage:

1. Big Data Analytics: It's a popular choice for storing data used in big data analytics pipelines, as it provides the required scale and performance.

2. Data Warehousing: Data Lake Storage can serve as a staging area for data ingested into data warehouses like Azure SQL Data Warehouse.

3. Data Lake and Data Warehouse Integration: You can use Data Lake Storage in conjunction with Azure services like Azure Databricks, Azure HDInsight, and Azure Synapse Analytics to process and analyze data.

Working with Azure Data Lake Storage:

1. Create an Azure Data Lake Storage Account: Start by creating a Data Lake Storage account in the Azure portal.

2. Uploading Data: Use Azure Storage Explorer, Azure Data Factory, or other Azure tools to upload data to your Data Lake Storage account.

3. Managing Data: Organize your data into folders and directories, apply access control, and take advantage of data partitioning and optimization for analytics.

4. Access and Analytics: Use Azure services like Azure Databricks, Azure HDInsight, or Azure Data Factory to process and analyze the data stored in Data Lake Storage.

5. Security and Compliance: Implement security measures, manage access, and comply with data governance standards.

Understanding Azure Data Lake Storage is fundamental to utilizing its capabilities for your data preparation and analytics needs. It provides the foundation for a scalable, secure, and flexible data storage solution within the Azure ecosystem.

Data Lake Storage Gen1 vs. Gen2

Azure Data Lake Storage Gen1 and Gen2 are both cloud-based storage solutions designed for big data analytics, but they differ in various aspects. Understanding their differences is essential for choosing the right solution for your specific use case.

Data Lake Storage Gen1:

1. Architecture: Gen1 is based on the Azure Data Lake Store and is designed for big data processing. It offers a distributed file system that can handle massive amounts of data.

2. File System: Gen1 uses a flat file system and is optimized for storing large unstructured or semi-structured data, such as log files and media files.

3. Performance: While Gen1 is suitable for big data workloads, its performance and analytics capabilities are not as advanced as Gen2.

4. Analytics: It provides basic analytics capabilities but may require additional services for more advanced analytics and processing.

Data Lake Storage Gen2:

1. Architecture: Gen2 builds on Azure Blob Storage, which is highly durable and scalable. It combines the capabilities of Azure Data Lake Store with Azure Blob Storage.

2. Hierarchical File System: Gen2 introduces a hierarchical file system, making it easier to organize data into folders and subfolders. This structure is more familiar to users and simplifies data management.

3. Performance: Gen2 offers improved performance, making it a better choice for modern data analytics workloads.

4. Security: It provides better integration with Azure Active Directory for fine-grained access control and security features, including encryption at rest and in transit.

5. Analytics: Gen2 is integrated with Azure Data Lake Analytics and supports advanced analytics and processing capabilities.

Choosing Between Gen1 and Gen2:

When deciding between Gen1 and Gen2, consider the following factors:

1. Use Case: Gen2 is recommended for most new projects due to its improved performance and hierarchical file system. However, Gen1 may be suitable if you have existing workloads.

2. Analytics Requirements: If your data analytics and processing needs are extensive, Gen2's integration with Azure Data Lake Analytics makes it a more suitable choice.

3. Data Structure: Gen2's hierarchical file system is more user-friendly and efficient for organizing data, especially if you have a large number of files.

4. Security: Gen2 offers better security features and Azure AD integration, which may be crucial for your organization's compliance requirements.

5. Migration: If you're migrating from Gen1 to Gen2, you can leverage Azure Data Factory or Azure Databricks to transition your data seamlessly.

In conclusion, Azure Data Lake Storage Gen2 is the preferred choice for most new big data projects due to its improved performance, hierarchical file system, and advanced analytics capabilities. However, Gen1 may still be relevant for legacy workloads or specific use cases.

Managing Data in Azure Data Lake Storage

Once data is stored in Azure Data Lake Storage, effective management is crucial to ensure that it's organized, secure, and accessible to users and applications. This section will guide you through managing data in Azure Data Lake Storage.

1. Organizing Data:

- **Folders and Directories:** Azure Data Lake Storage allows you to organize data into folders and subfolders. A well-structured hierarchy can make it easier to locate and manage files.

- **File Naming Conventions:** Implement consistent file naming conventions. Descriptive and standardized names help users understand the content of files.

2. Access Control and Security:

- **Azure Active Directory (Azure AD) Integration:** To control access to data, integrate Azure Data Lake Storage with Azure AD. This allows for role-based access control and fine-grained permissions.

- **Shared Access Signatures (SAS):** Use SAS tokens to provide time-limited, secure access to specific resources without exposing storage account keys.

3. Data Lifecycle Management:

- **Data Retention Policies:** Implement data retention policies to automatically delete or archive data after a specified period. This helps manage storage costs.

- **Data Archiving:** For data that needs to be preserved but not frequently accessed, consider moving it to a more cost-effective storage tier.

4. Monitoring and Logging:

- **Azure Monitor and Azure Security Center:** Set up monitoring and alerts using Azure Monitor to track the performance and health of your data lake storage.

- **Audit Logging:** Enable audit logging to capture activities and changes to data, ensuring compliance with regulations.

5. Data Transfer and Export:

- **Azure Data Factory:** Utilize Azure Data Factory for orchestrating data transfer between on-premises sources, cloud sources, and Azure Data Lake Storage.

- **Data Export:** Export data to other services, databases, or applications for further processing or analysis.

6. Data Backup:

- **Azure Backup:** Implement data backup solutions to protect against data loss or accidental deletion. Azure Backup can be used for this purpose.

7. Data Versioning:

- **Data Lake Storage Gen2:** Data Lake Storage Gen2 supports hierarchical namespaces and can assist in managing data versions by allowing overwrites, appends, and renames.

8. Data Purge Policies:

- **Automated Deletion:** Implement policies for automated data deletion or purging based on retention requirements and compliance.

Managing data in Azure Data Lake Storage is a crucial aspect of maintaining data quality, security, and efficiency. It ensures that data remains accessible, organized, and meets compliance standards. By following best practices for data management, you can harness the full potential of your data lake.

For more detailed instructions and examples related to data management in Azure Data Lake Storage, refer to the Azure documentation or contact Microsoft support if you encounter specific challenges.

4.3 Azure SQL Data Warehouse: A Scalable Data Warehouse

Introduction to Azure SQL Data Warehouse

Azure SQL Data Warehouse is a powerful, cloud-based, and fully managed analytical data warehouse service provided by Microsoft Azure. It's designed to handle large volumes of data and complex queries, making it an ideal choice for organizations seeking scalable data warehousing solutions. This section provides a comprehensive introduction to Azure SQL Data Warehouse.

1. Key Features and Benefits:

- **Massively Parallel Processing (MPP):** Azure SQL Data Warehouse uses a distributed architecture that leverages multiple compute nodes to parallelize and speed up query processing.

- **Scalability:** One of the significant advantages is its scalability. You can start with a small data warehouse and then scale up or down based on your requirements.

- **Integration:** It seamlessly integrates with other Azure services, such as Azure Data Factory and Azure Data Lake Storage, allowing you to create end-to-end data pipelines.

- **Security and Compliance:** Azure SQL Data Warehouse offers robust security features, including data encryption at rest and in transit. It's also compliant with various industry standards.

- **Columnstore Indexes:** It supports columnstore indexes, which are highly efficient for analytical workloads, speeding up query performance.

2. Data Warehousing Concepts:

   - **Star and Snowflake Schema:** Azure SQL Data Warehouse supports traditional star and snowflake schemas for structuring data.

   - **Facts and Dimensions:** Understanding facts (measures) and dimensions (attributes) is fundamental for designing your data warehouse schema.

   - **ETL Processes:** Azure SQL Data Warehouse is often used in conjunction with Extract, Transform, Load (ETL) processes to move, clean, and transform data.

3. Provisioning and Configuration:

   - **Service Tiers:** Azure SQL Data Warehouse offers various service tiers, including Gen2, which provides a higher level of performance and flexibility.

   - **Optimizing Query Performance:** Strategies for optimizing query performance, such as creating distribution keys and designing effective indexes.

4. Data Distribution and Scaling:

   - **Data Distribution:** Understanding how data is distributed across compute nodes in Azure SQL Data Warehouse is crucial for optimal query performance.

   - **Scaling Compute Resources:** You can dynamically allocate more or fewer compute resources based on the workloads, ensuring cost-efficiency.

5. Data Loading and Querying:

- **Loading Data:** Guidance on loading data into Azure SQL Data Warehouse, including best practices for bulk loading.

- **Querying Data:** An overview of querying data using T-SQL, including complex queries and data exploration.

6. Use Cases and Applications:

- **Business Intelligence:** Azure SQL Data Warehouse is often used as the backend for business intelligence tools like Power BI for data reporting and visualization.

- **Data Analytics:** It supports advanced analytics, machine learning, and data mining on large datasets.

- **Real-time Analytics:** For scenarios where real-time data analysis is required.

This introduction lays the foundation for exploring Azure SQL Data Warehouse in more detail. As you proceed, you'll learn how to provision and configure your data warehouse, design effective schemas, and manage its performance for data warehousing and analytical workloads.

Data Warehousing Concepts

In the world of data warehousing, understanding the foundational concepts is essential for designing an effective and efficient data warehouse. Here, we'll delve into some of the fundamental concepts that play a pivotal role in shaping your data warehousing solution within Azure SQL Data Warehouse.

1. Star and Snowflake Schema:

   - **Star Schema:** The star schema is a common approach for structuring data in a data warehouse. In this schema, you have a central fact table containing measures (numeric data like sales, revenue, etc.), and surrounding it are dimension tables with attributes (e.g., time, product, location). The fact table is connected to dimension tables through foreign keys.

   - **Snowflake Schema:** The snowflake schema is an extension of the star schema. In this schema, dimension tables are normalized, meaning that hierarchies are separated into different tables. It can help reduce redundancy but might result in more complex queries.

2. Facts and Dimensions:

   - **Facts:** In a data warehouse, facts represent the measurable data, typically numeric, that you want to analyze. These are often referred to as measures. For instance, in a retail data warehouse, facts could include sales revenue, quantity sold, or profit.

   - **Dimensions:** Dimensions are the descriptive attributes that provide context to the facts. They are often non-numeric and include attributes like time, product, customer, or location. Dimensions help users to filter, slice, and dice data for analysis.

3. ETL Processes:

   - **Extract:** Data from various sources is extracted and transferred to a staging area in Azure SQL Data Warehouse.

   - **Transform:** Data is cleansed, enriched, and transformed to suit the data warehouse schema. This process may involve data quality checks, aggregations, and data type conversions.

- **Load:** The transformed data is loaded into the data warehouse. Loading strategies can vary, including incremental loading and bulk loading.

4. Hierarchies:

- Hierarchies are used to organize dimension attributes in a structured way. For example, a time dimension could have hierarchies for year, quarter, month, and day.

5. Slowly Changing Dimensions:

- Slowly changing dimensions (SCDs) are dimensions where attributes can change over time. There are different types of SCDs, and understanding how to handle them is critical in maintaining historical data accurately.

6. Surrogate Keys:

- Surrogate keys are system-generated keys assigned to dimension tables. They help in uniquely identifying rows even when natural keys change.

7. Type 2 Dimensions:

- Type 2 dimensions are used to track historical changes to dimension attributes. They create a new row with updated attributes when changes occur.

8. Data Mart vs. Data Warehouse:

- A data warehouse often feeds data marts, which are smaller subsets of the data warehouse tailored for specific business units or departments. Data marts are optimized for the needs of their users.

Understanding these concepts is crucial for designing a data warehousing solution within Azure SQL Data Warehouse. Proper schema design, effective ETL processes, and understanding your data's nature (facts and dimensions) are essential for building a data warehouse that supports efficient and meaningful analytics.

Data Distribution and Scaling in Azure SQL Data Warehouse

In Azure SQL Data Warehouse, data distribution and scaling play a pivotal role in optimizing performance and making the most out of your data warehousing solution. Let's dive into these two crucial aspects.

Data Distribution:

Data distribution refers to the way data is physically stored and organized across nodes (or distributions) in your Azure SQL Data Warehouse. There are two main distribution methods: hash distribution and round-robin distribution.

1. Hash Distribution:

- In this method, rows are distributed across distributions based on a hash of one or more columns. Each distribution holds a subset of the data, and the distribution key is used to ensure that rows with the same hash value are stored on the same distribution. This is useful for scenarios where you have a natural distribution key, such as customer ID, which is frequently used in join operations.

- Hash distribution minimizes data movement during queries since it keeps related data on the same distribution.

- However, if the distribution key is not chosen wisely, it may lead to data skew, where some distributions have significantly more data than others.

- For example, if you distribute sales data by the customer ID, all sales data for a particular customer will reside on a single distribution.

2. Round-Robin Distribution:

- In this method, data is distributed uniformly across distributions in a round-robin fashion. This is a good choice when you don't have a clear distribution key and want to ensure data is evenly spread across distributions.

- Round-robin distribution can lead to better load performance since data is evenly loaded into all distributions.

- However, it might lead to data shuffling during queries, which can impact query performance for large datasets.

Scaling:

Azure SQL Data Warehouse allows you to easily scale your resources to handle the specific needs of your workload. Scaling in Azure SQL Data Warehouse is achieved through Data Warehouse Units (DWUs). DWUs represent a measure of compute capacity. You can increase or decrease the number of DWUs to match your workload requirements.

- **Scaling Up:** Increasing the number of DWUs provides more compute power, which can significantly improve query performance for complex workloads.

- **Scaling Down:** Reducing the number of DWUs can help you save costs when you have less intensive workloads.

- **Pause/Resume:** You can also pause your Azure SQL Data Warehouse during periods of inactivity to save costs. When you're ready to use it again, you can easily resume it.

It's important to choose the right data distribution method and scaling level based on your specific use case and workload. Keep in mind that performance optimization often involves a balance between data distribution, scaling, and query design.

For example, a query that frequently joins two large tables might benefit from using hash distribution based on the join key, while a data loading process might benefit from round-robin distribution to achieve even data distribution during loading.

If you're working with Azure SQL Data Warehouse and want to ensure optimal performance, it's crucial to monitor query performance and adjust your distribution and scaling settings as needed.

CHAPTER IV
Integrating Power BI with Azure Data Services

5.1 Connecting Power BI to Azure Data Sources

Configuring Data Source Connections in Power BI

Configuring data source connections is a fundamental step in creating reports and dashboards in Power BI. It enables Power BI to connect to your data stored in various Azure services. Let's delve into the process of configuring data source connections in Power BI.

1. Launch Power BI Desktop:

  - To configure data source connections, start by opening Power BI Desktop on your local machine.

2. Get Data:

  - Once you have Power BI Desktop open, click on the "Get Data" button located on the Home tab of the Power BI ribbon.

3. Choose Data Source:

- A window will appear with a list of data sources you can connect to. Depending on your Azure data source, select the appropriate one.

- For example, if you want to connect to Azure SQL Data Warehouse, choose "Azure" and then select "Azure SQL Data Warehouse." If you're connecting to Azure Blob Storage, choose "Azure" and select "Azure Blob Storage."

4. Connection Settings:

- After selecting your data source, you will need to provide connection details. This usually includes the server address, database name, authentication method, and credentials.

- If you're connecting to Azure services, you will typically use Azure Active Directory (Azure AD) credentials for authentication.

5. Advanced Options (Optional):

- Depending on the data source, you may have advanced options to configure, such as specifying a query or filtering options.

- For Azure services like Azure SQL Data Warehouse, you can specify a SQL statement or use the Power Query Editor to transform and filter the data.

6. Test Connection:

- To ensure that your connection settings are correct, you can use the "Test Connection" button (if available). This will verify that Power BI can successfully connect to your data source.

7. Load Data:

- Once you've configured the connection settings, click the "Load" button to bring the data into Power BI.

- Depending on the data source size and complexity, it might take some time to load the data into Power BI.

8. Data Transformation and Modeling:

- After loading the data, you can use Power Query to perform data transformation and modeling. This step is crucial for preparing the data for creating reports and dashboards.

9. Create Reports and Dashboards:

- With your data loaded and transformed, you can proceed to create reports and dashboards in Power BI using the Power BI Desktop's user-friendly interface.

10. Publish to Power BI Service (Optional):

- Once your report is ready, you can publish it to the Power BI service, which allows for sharing and collaboration with others in your organization.

By following these steps, you can configure data source connections in Power BI and start building insightful reports and dashboards using your data from Azure services. Remember that the specific configuration details may vary depending on the data source, so ensure you have the necessary connection information at hand.

Importing Data from Azure Blob Storage

Azure Blob Storage is a powerful cloud-based object storage solution provided by Microsoft Azure. You can easily import data from Azure Blob Storage into Power BI for analysis and reporting. Here's how to import data from Azure Blob Storage into Power BI:

1. Launch Power BI Desktop:

- Start by opening Power BI Desktop on your local machine.

2. Get Data:

- Click on the "Get Data" button in the Home tab of the Power BI ribbon.

3. Select Azure -> Azure Blob Storage:

- In the "Get Data" window, scroll down and select "Azure" as the data source category.

- Choose "Azure Blob Storage" from the list of available connectors and click "Connect."

4. Provide Azure Blob Storage Account Details:

- A dialog will appear where you need to enter the details of your Azure Blob Storage account:

  - **Account name:** Enter the name of your Azure Blob Storage account.

  - **Container name:** Specify the name of the container from which you want to import data.

  - **Access level:** Choose the access level for the container (e.g., "Blob" or "Container" level).

- Click "OK" after entering the details.

5. Navigator Window:

- The Navigator window will open, displaying a list of available tables or files in the selected container. You can preview and select the tables or files you want to import.

6. Data Load Options:

- Choose whether you want to load the data into Power BI by clicking the "Load" button or transform the data using Power Query by clicking the "Transform data" button.

- If you click "Load," the data will be imported as-is into Power BI. If you click "Transform data," you'll have the opportunity to perform data cleaning, transformations, and shaping using Power Query.

7. Data Transformation and Modeling (if using Power Query):

- If you selected "Transform data," the Power Query Editor will open, allowing you to perform data transformations and modeling on the imported data.

8. Load Data into Power BI:

- Once you've reviewed and transformed the data (if necessary), click the "Close & Apply" button in Power Query to load the data into Power BI.

9. Create Reports and Dashboards:

- Now that your data is in Power BI, you can start creating reports and dashboards using the Power BI Desktop's user-friendly interface.

10. Publish to Power BI Service (Optional):

- If you want to share your reports and dashboards with others in your organization, you can publish them to the Power BI service.

By following these steps, you can easily import data from Azure Blob Storage into Power BI. This process is essential for building insightful reports and dashboards using data stored in Azure Blob Storage.

DirectQuery and Live Connection to Azure SQL Data Warehouse

Power BI offers two primary methods to connect to data sources: Import and DirectQuery. In the case of Azure SQL Data Warehouse, you can use DirectQuery or Live Connection to establish a connection. Let's explore how to set up DirectQuery and Live Connection to Azure SQL Data Warehouse in Power BI:

DirectQuery:

DirectQuery is a method to connect Power BI directly to a data source, such as Azure SQL Data Warehouse, in a way that queries are sent directly to the database. It is particularly useful when dealing with large datasets or when you need real-time data without importing it into Power BI. Here's how to set up DirectQuery:

1. Launch Power BI Desktop:

- Open Power BI Desktop on your local machine.

2. Get Data:

- Click on the "Get Data" button in the Home tab of the Power BI ribbon.

3. Select Database -> Azure -> Azure SQL Data Warehouse:

- In the "Get Data" window, choose "Database" as the data source category.

- Select "Azure" and then "Azure SQL Data Warehouse."

- Click "Connect."

4. Provide Connection Details:

- In the next window, enter the necessary connection details for your Azure SQL Data Warehouse:

- **Server:** The server name of your Azure SQL Data Warehouse.

- **Database:** Name of the database you want to connect to.

- **Authentication:** Choose how you want to authenticate (e.g., Windows or Database).

5. Load Data:

- After entering the connection details, you'll see a "DirectQuery" option. Select this option if you want to use DirectQuery.

- Click "OK."

6. Query Editor (Optional):

- The Power Query Editor will open if you need to perform data transformations or apply filters to the data. This is optional when using DirectQuery.

7. Create Reports:

- Now you can start creating reports and dashboards using the Azure SQL Data Warehouse data. All the querying happens directly on the database server.

Live Connection:

A Live Connection in Power BI establishes a connection to Azure SQL Data Warehouse, but it does allow you to import a subset of data for quick report generation. When you use a Live Connection, any changes in the data are reflected in real-time.

To set up a Live Connection:

1. Follow the same steps as for DirectQuery up to the "DirectQuery" option.

2. Instead of choosing DirectQuery, select "Import."

3. Load a subset of data for report building. Any changes in the underlying data in Azure SQL Data Warehouse are reflected in the Power BI reports in real-time.

Both DirectQuery and Live Connection provide real-time access to your Azure SQL Data Warehouse data. Your choice depends on your specific requirements and whether you want to perform transformations in Power Query or directly in the database. These methods help you create interactive and responsive reports with data from Azure SQL Data Warehouse.

5.2 Data Modeling and Transformation in Power BI

Building Data Models in Power BI Desktop

In Power BI, creating robust and efficient data models is crucial for building meaningful reports and visualizations. A data model defines the relationships between tables and the structure of your data. Let's go through the steps to build data models in Power BI Desktop:

1. Import Data:

- Launch Power BI Desktop and select "Get Data" from the Home tab.

- Choose your data source, like Azure SQL Data Warehouse, and connect to it. You can also import data from various sources, including Excel, CSV files, and more.

2. Data Transformation:

- After connecting to your data source, you may need to transform the data in the Power Query Editor.

- You can access the Power Query Editor by clicking "Edit Queries" from the Home tab.

- In the Power Query Editor, you can perform tasks like filtering rows, removing duplicates, transforming data types, and merging tables.

3. Create Relationships:

- In Power BI Desktop, you can define relationships between tables. This is critical for building data models.

- Go to the "Model" view by clicking the "Model" icon on the left-hand side.

- In the Model view, you can see all the tables imported from your data source.

- To create relationships, drag and drop fields between related tables. Power BI will automatically detect and suggest relationships based on column names, but you can also customize these relationships.

4. Define Measures and Calculated Columns:

- Measures are calculated values based on your data. They are often used for calculations like sums, averages, or ratios.

- Calculated columns allow you to create new columns based on expressions you define.

- You can define both measures and calculated columns in the "Modeling" tab in Power BI Desktop.

5. Optimize for Performance:

- To ensure your report loads quickly and efficiently, consider using techniques like creating summary tables, hiding unnecessary columns, and optimizing your data model.

- You can use the "Manage Relationships" window to manage relationships effectively.

6. Test and Iterate:

- Build visuals and reports in the "Report" view to test your data model.

- Make sure the relationships, measures, and calculations work as expected.

- Iteratively refine your data model as you create reports.

7. Publish to Power BI Service:

- Once you are satisfied with your data model and reports, you can publish your report to the Power BI Service.

- The Power BI Service provides a cloud-based platform for sharing and collaborating on your reports.

Remember that a well-structured data model is the foundation for creating powerful and insightful reports in Power BI. It's essential to understand your data source, the relationships between tables, and the calculations you need to perform. With a solid data model in place, you can create compelling visualizations and gain valuable insights from your data.

Data Shaping with Power Query Editor

Power Query Editor in Power BI is a powerful tool for shaping and transforming your data. It allows you to clean, reshape, and prepare your data for analysis and reporting. Here's a detailed guide on how to shape data using Power Query Editor:

1. Accessing Power Query Editor:

- In Power BI Desktop, load your data source by clicking on "Get Data" in the Home tab and selecting your source (e.g., Azure SQL Data Warehouse).

- Once you've loaded the data, choose "Edit Queries" from the Home tab to open Power Query Editor.

2. Navigating Power Query Editor:

- The Power Query Editor interface is divided into several sections:

  - **Queries:** Lists all the queries you have created.

  - **Query Settings:** Displays query-specific settings and transformations.

  - **Preview:** Provides a preview of your data at each step of transformation.

  - **Query Dependencies:** Shows dependencies between queries.

  - **Applied Steps:** Lists all the applied transformation steps.

3. Basic Data Transformations:

- You can perform basic transformations such as filtering rows, sorting, and renaming columns directly from the Power Query Editor.

- To filter rows, click on the filter icon in the column header and set the desired criteria.

- To sort columns, right-click on the column header and choose "Sort Ascending" or "Sort Descending."

- To rename a column, right-click on the column header and select "Rename."

4. Advanced Transformations:

- Power Query Editor offers advanced transformations that are especially useful for data shaping:

   - **Splitting Columns:** You can split a column into multiple columns based on delimiters or specific positions within the text.

   - **Pivoting and Unpivoting:** Transform data from wide to long format and vice versa.

   - **Merging Queries:** Combine data from multiple queries into a single query.

   - **Data Type Conversions:** Change the data type of columns.

   - **Adding Custom Columns:** Create new columns with custom expressions.

   - **Grouping and Aggregation:** Group data and perform aggregations.

   - **Conditional Columns:** Create columns based on conditional logic.

5. Applied Steps:

- Power Query Editor keeps track of all the applied transformations in the "Applied Steps" section.

- You can see a step-by-step history of the data shaping process and edit or delete steps if needed.

6. Preview and Load:

- Use the "Preview" section to see the results of your data shaping as you apply transformations.

- When you're satisfied with the data, click "Close & Apply" to load the transformed data into Power BI.

7. Refresh Data:

- Power BI allows you to set up data refresh schedules to keep your data up to date automatically.

8. Error Handling:

- Power Query Editor provides error-handling options, such as replacing errors with custom values or ignoring errors during data loading.

By using Power Query Editor effectively, you can clean, reshape, and prepare your data for analysis. It's a versatile tool for handling a wide range of data transformation tasks, and it significantly improves the quality and usability of your datasets. Don't hesitate to use the advanced transformation options to achieve the desired structure and format for your data.

Advanced Data Transformation Techniques

In Power BI, advanced data transformation techniques are crucial for preparing your data for meaningful analysis and visualization. These techniques go beyond basic data shaping and include more complex operations to ensure your data is accurate and insightful. Here's a detailed guide on using advanced data transformation techniques in Power BI:

1. Merging Queries:

- Merging queries allows you to combine data from multiple sources. This is particularly useful when you have related data in different tables.

- To merge queries, you can use the "Merge Queries" option in the Power Query Editor.

- Choose the type of join (e.g., inner join, left outer join) and specify the join columns.

- The result is a single query that combines data from the merged queries.

2. Grouping and Aggregation:

- Grouping and aggregation are essential for summarizing data, calculating totals, or creating aggregated measures for analysis.

- You can group data by one or more columns and apply aggregation functions (e.g., sum, count, average) to each group.

- Grouped data can be further used in visualizations, making it easier to understand trends and patterns.

3. Conditional Columns:

- Conditional columns allow you to create new columns based on specific conditions.

- For example, you can create a column that classifies data into categories based on a numerical value or a text column.

- Use conditional statements like "if," "else if," and "else" to define the logic for the new column.

4. Custom Functions:

- Power Query in Power BI allows you to create custom functions in the M language.

- Custom functions can be reused across multiple queries and offer a way to encapsulate complex data transformation logic.

- You can define parameters for your functions to make them more flexible and versatile.

5. Pivot and Unpivot:

- Pivoting and unpivoting data is useful when you need to reshape your data from a wide format (e.g., with columns for each time period) to a long format (e.g., with rows for each time period).

- These operations can be done directly in the Power Query Editor.

6. Data Type Conversions:

- Ensure that your data has the correct data types to enable meaningful calculations and visualizations.

- You can change data types for columns, which may involve converting text to numbers, or vice versa.

7. Error Handling:

- When dealing with data from different sources, you might encounter errors or inconsistencies.

- Power Query Editor provides options for handling errors, such as replacing errors with custom values or ignoring them during data loading.

8. Parameterization:

- Parameterization enables you to create dynamic queries that can be easily adjusted for different scenarios.

- Parameters can be used for various purposes, including changing data source paths, filtering data, or specifying date ranges.

9. Recursive Functions:

- Recursive functions allow you to apply transformations iteratively to hierarchical data structures or create running totals.

- They are written in the M language and can be powerful for solving complex data transformation challenges.

10. Leveraging Custom Columns and Measures:

- Create custom columns and measures using the DAX (Data Analysis Expressions) language to perform calculations and aggregations that are specific to your business requirements.

11. Testing and Iteration:

- When applying advanced data transformations, it's crucial to test and iterate to ensure that the results are as expected.

Using these advanced data transformation techniques in Power BI will help you transform raw data into valuable insights for reporting and visualization. These techniques empower you to perform complex operations on your data and create custom solutions that cater to your specific business needs.

5.3 Real-time Data Streaming with Azure Stream Analytics

Introduction to Azure Stream Analytics

Azure Stream Analytics is a real-time data stream processing service offered by Microsoft Azure. It is designed for processing and analyzing high volumes of real-time data streams from various sources. In this section, we'll provide a detailed introduction to Azure Stream Analytics and how it can be used in conjunction with Power BI for real-time reporting.

Key Concepts and Components:

1. Data Ingestion: Azure Stream Analytics enables the ingestion of data from a wide range of sources, including IoT devices, applications, logs, and more. It supports both structured and semi-structured data.

2. Real-Time Data Processing: Stream Analytics processes incoming data in real-time. It allows you to perform filtering, transformations, and enrichments on the data as it flows through the system.

3. SQL-Like Query Language: Stream Analytics provides a SQL-like query language for defining transformations and analytics on streaming data. This language is used to create queries that specify how data should be processed.

4. Input and Output: The service allows you to define input sources (e.g., Azure Event Hubs, Azure IoT Hub, Azure Blob Storage, or custom endpoints) and output sinks (e.g., Azure SQL Database, Azure Cosmos DB, Power BI, or custom destinations).

5. Temporal Operations: You can work with temporal windows and time-based operations to perform tasks like tumbling, hopping, and sliding window aggregations.

6. Integration with Power BI: One of the key features is its ability to integrate with Power BI for real-time reporting. Data processed by Stream Analytics can be visualized in Power BI dashboards and reports to provide real-time insights.

Use Cases:

Azure Stream Analytics is well-suited for a variety of real-time data processing scenarios, including:

- **IoT Data Processing:** Analyzing data generated by IoT devices to monitor device health, detect anomalies, and trigger alerts.

- **Application Monitoring:** Capturing and analyzing application logs and telemetry in real-time.

- **Social Media Analysis:** Analyzing social media feeds for trends, sentiment analysis, and engagement metrics.

- **Fraud Detection:** Identifying fraudulent transactions or activities as they occur.

- **Real-Time Analytics:** Enabling real-time dashboards and reports for monitoring key performance indicators.

Getting Started:

To start using Azure Stream Analytics:

1. Azure Portal: Create an Azure Stream Analytics job using the Azure Portal and configure your inputs and outputs.

2. Query Language: Write Stream Analytics queries using the SQL-like language to define how data should be processed.

3. Integration with Power BI: Set up the integration between Azure Stream Analytics and Power BI to enable real-time reporting.

Benefits:

- Real-time Processing: Stream Analytics provides low-latency, real-time processing capabilities.

- Scalability: It can scale based on the volume of incoming data.

- Integration: Seamless integration with various Azure services and Power BI for real-time reporting.

- User-Friendly: Its SQL-like query language makes it accessible to users with SQL skills.

Next Steps:

The next section will focus on setting up Stream Analytics jobs, configuring inputs and outputs, and performing data transformations using the Stream Analytics query language. We'll also explore how to integrate Stream Analytics with Power BI for real-time reporting.

Setting Up Stream Analytics Jobs

Setting up Azure Stream Analytics jobs is a fundamental step in processing and analyzing real-time data streams. This section will walk you through the process of creating and configuring Stream Analytics jobs in Azure.

Step 1: Create a Stream Analytics Job

1. Azure Portal: Log in to the Azure Portal and navigate to the "Create a resource" option.

2. Search for "Stream Analytics Job": In the Azure Marketplace, search for "Stream Analytics Job" and select it.

3. Job Configuration: Provide a unique job name, select the Azure subscription, create or select a resource group, and choose the location. Click "Review + create" to validate the configuration.

4. Validation and Creation: After validation, click "Create" to create the Stream Analytics job.

Step 2: Define Inputs

Inputs are the sources from which Azure Stream Analytics ingests data. Here's how to set up an input:

1. Select "Inputs": In your Stream Analytics job overview, select "Inputs."

2. Add an Input: Click "Add" to create a new input.

3. Input Type: Choose the type of input source. Common sources include Azure Event Hubs, Azure IoT Hub, Blob storage, and more.

4. Input Details: Configure the details of the input source, such as providing the connection string, event hub namespace, or IoT hub endpoint.

5. Schema and Serialization: Define the input schema and specify the serialization format (e.g., JSON, Avro).

Step 3: Define Outputs

Outputs are destinations where processed data will be sent. Here's how to configure outputs:

1. **Select "Outputs":** In your Stream Analytics job overview, select "Outputs."

2. **Add an Output:** Click "Add" to create a new output.

3. **Output Type:** Choose the type of output destination. Common destinations include Azure SQL Database, Azure Cosmos DB, Power BI, and more.

4. **Output Details:** Configure the details of the output destination, such as connection strings and table or container names.

5. **Output Serialization:** Specify how data should be serialized for the output. For example, choose the format for writing data to SQL Database.

Step 4: Define Query

Azure Stream Analytics uses a SQL-like query language for data transformations. Define your query:

1. **Select "Query":** In your Stream Analytics job overview, select "Query."

2. **Write Query:** Use the query editor to write SQL-like queries to transform and process incoming data. For example, you can filter, aggregate, and enrich data.

3. Test Query: Use the query testing feature to validate your query with sample data.

Step 5: Start the Job

Once you've configured inputs, outputs, and the query, it's time to start the Stream Analytics job:

1. Save Your Changes: Ensure you save your job configuration.

2. Start the Job: Click "Start" to initiate the job. Stream Analytics will begin processing data in real-time based on your configuration.

Monitoring and Optimization:

- Azure Stream Analytics provides monitoring and diagnostic features, allowing you to track job performance and troubleshoot any issues.

- Optimize queries and configurations for efficient data processing.

In the next section, we will explore the process of integrating Azure Stream Analytics with Power BI for real-time reporting, allowing you to visualize the processed data in Power BI dashboards and reports.

Integrating Stream Analytics with Power BI for Real-time Reporting

Integrating Azure Stream Analytics with Power BI enables you to create real-time reports and dashboards that reflect the insights derived from streaming data. In this section, we'll explore the process of integrating Azure Stream Analytics with Power BI for real-time reporting.

Step 1: Stream Analytics Job Output to Power BI

1. Stream Analytics Output Configuration: In your Azure Stream Analytics job, configure the output to send data to Power BI. This is typically done in the "Outputs" section of your Stream Analytics job. Select "Power BI" as the output type.

2. Power BI Configuration: Configure the Power BI output by specifying the workspace name and dataset name. You will need to authenticate and authorize Stream Analytics to write to your Power BI workspace.

3. Data Mapping: Define the mapping between the fields in your Stream Analytics query output and the datasets, tables, and columns in your Power BI workspace.

Step 2: Real-time Dashboard Creation in Power BI

1. Power BI Desktop: Open Power BI Desktop, the tool for creating reports and dashboards.

2. Data Source Connection: Create a new report, and connect to the Power BI dataset that is linked to your Stream Analytics job.

3. Real-time Data Visualizations: Build real-time visualizations using Power BI components like live tiles, streaming visuals, and line charts.

4. Real-time Refresh: Ensure that your report is set to use real-time data. Configure the refresh rate according to your requirements.

5. Dashboard Design: Design your Power BI dashboard to display real-time insights. You can add tiles, tables, charts, and other visual elements.

6. Publish to Power BI Service: After creating the report in Power BI Desktop, publish it to the Power BI service. You can share it with colleagues or embed it in web applications.

Step 3: Real-time Monitoring

With the integration of Azure Stream Analytics and Power BI, you can continuously monitor real-time data streams and make data-driven decisions. Some aspects of real-time monitoring include:

- **Threshold Alerts:** Set up threshold alerts within Power BI to trigger notifications when specific conditions are met or exceeded.

- **Historical Analysis:** Combine real-time dashboards with historical data for comprehensive analysis.

- **Collaboration:** Share the real-time dashboard with your team to foster collaboration and informed decision-making.

Step 4: Continuous Optimization

Continuously optimize your Stream Analytics job and Power BI reports:

- **Stream Analytics Query:** Refine your Stream Analytics query for better data transformations and filtering.

- **Performance:** Monitor the performance of your real-time reports and dashboards to ensure efficient data processing.

- **User Feedback:** Gather feedback from users to improve the effectiveness of your real-time reporting solution.

Security Considerations: Ensure that you follow best practices for securing your Stream Analytics job and Power BI datasets. This includes data encryption, authentication, and access control.

By following these steps and best practices, you can successfully integrate Azure Stream Analytics with Power BI for real-time reporting, enabling your organization to gain insights from streaming data and make informed decisions in real time.

CHAPTER V
Advanced Analytics with Azure Machine Learning

6.1 Introduction to Azure Machine Learning

Understanding Azure Machine Learning Services

Azure Machine Learning is a comprehensive cloud-based platform that provides tools, services, and environments for building, training, and deploying machine learning models. In this section, we will delve into an understanding of Azure Machine Learning Services and its key components.

Azure Machine Learning Components

Azure Machine Learning is composed of several key components:

1. Azure Machine Learning Workspace: The workspace serves as the top-level resource for the machine learning service. It provides a centralized place to work with your machine learning assets like datasets, models, and deployments. You can create multiple workspaces within your Azure subscription.

2. Experiment: An experiment is a project within your workspace where you develop, train, and evaluate machine learning models. It's where you organize and keep track of your work, including data, code, and model versions.

3. Datasets: Datasets are a core component of machine learning. Azure Machine Learning allows you to easily discover, access, and manage datasets. You can use data from a variety of sources, including Azure Blob Storage and Azure SQL Database.

4. Compute Targets: These are the resources that you use to run your machine learning workloads, such as model training. Azure Machine Learning supports various compute targets, including Azure Machine Learning Compute (a managed service for training), Azure Kubernetes Service, and more.

5. Machine Learning Models: You can develop, train, and manage machine learning models within the workspace. Azure Machine Learning provides tools to streamline the model training process.

6. Notebooks: Notebooks provide an interactive environment for writing, running, and sharing code. Azure Machine Learning supports Jupyter notebooks, which are commonly used for data exploration, model development, and experimentation.

7. Pipelines: Machine learning pipelines enable you to create and manage end-to-end workflows that automate model training, deployment, and monitoring. You can schedule and run these pipelines as needed.

8. Environments: Environments define the execution context for your code and dependencies. You can create reusable environments to ensure consistent and reproducible runs across different compute targets.

The Machine Learning Process

The process of working with Azure Machine Learning generally involves the following steps:

1. Data Preparation: This step involves collecting, cleaning, and transforming your data. You can use Azure Machine Learning's data management capabilities to assist with these tasks.

2. Experimentation: Create experiments to develop and train your machine learning models. These experiments allow you to track your work, compare models, and make improvements.

3. Model Deployment: Once you have a trained model that meets your requirements, you can deploy it as a web service or container for integration into applications.

4. Model Monitoring and Maintenance: Continuously monitor your deployed models to ensure they perform well over time. If necessary, retrain and redeploy models to maintain their accuracy.

Building Predictive Models with Azure ML

Azure Machine Learning provides a variety of tools for building predictive models. You can use popular machine learning libraries like scikit-learn, TensorFlow, and PyTorch, or take advantage of automated machine learning (AutoML) to accelerate the model-building process.

Code Illustration (Python)

Here's a simplified example of training a machine learning model using Azure Machine Learning with Python:

```python
from azureml.core import Experiment, Workspace
from azureml.train.sklearn import SKLearn
```

```python
from azureml.core.authentication import InteractiveLoginAuthentication

# Authenticate to your Azure Machine Learning workspace
interactive_auth = InteractiveLoginAuthentication(tenant_id="YOUR_TENANT_ID")
ws = Workspace.get(name="YOUR_WORKSPACE_NAME", auth=interactive_auth,
subscription_id="YOUR_SUBSCRIPTION_ID")

# Create an experiment
experiment = Experiment(workspace=ws, name="my-experiment")

# Specify a training script
est = SKLearn(source_directory=".", entry_script="train.py", compute_target="local")

# Start training
run = experiment.submit(est)
run.wait_for_completion(show_output=True)
```

This code demonstrates how to authenticate, set up an experiment, define a compute target, and initiate model training.

Understanding Azure Machine Learning Services and its components is crucial for efficiently developing and deploying machine learning solutions on the Azure platform. In the subsequent sections, we will explore the machine learning process and delve into building predictive models in more detail.

The Machine Learning Process

The machine learning process in Azure Machine Learning involves several key stages, which are essential for developing, training, and deploying machine learning models. Let's explore these stages in detail.

1. Data Preparation:

Data is the foundation of any machine learning project. In this initial stage, you collect, clean, and preprocess your data. Azure Machine Learning offers various data management capabilities, including data ingestion from different sources, data transformation, and data labeling. Data preparation is a crucial step, as the quality and suitability of your data greatly impact the performance of your machine learning models.

2. Data Exploration:

Before diving into model development, it's essential to gain a deep understanding of your data. Exploratory data analysis (EDA) helps you identify patterns, anomalies, and relationships within the data. Tools like Jupyter notebooks in Azure Machine Learning can be used for data exploration.

3. Feature Engineering:

Feature engineering involves selecting and creating relevant features from your data. This step helps improve the predictive power of your machine learning models. Azure Machine Learning provides tools for feature selection, extraction, and transformation.

4. Model Development:

This stage is where you create and train machine learning models using your prepared data. Azure Machine Learning supports a wide range of machine learning frameworks and libraries, such as scikit-learn, TensorFlow, PyTorch, and more. You can also take advantage of automated machine learning (AutoML) to streamline model development.

5. Model Evaluation:

After training your machine learning models, you need to assess their performance. Azure Machine Learning offers metrics, logging, and visualization tools to help you evaluate your models' accuracy, precision, recall, and other relevant metrics.

6. Hyperparameter Tuning:

Fine-tuning model hyperparameters is a critical part of the process. Azure Machine Learning supports hyperparameter optimization techniques that automatically search for the best combination of hyperparameters to optimize model performance.

7. Model Deployment:

Once you have a trained model that meets your requirements, it's time to deploy it. Azure Machine Learning allows you to deploy models as web services or containers. These deployed models can be integrated into applications, services, and dashboards for real-time predictions.

8. Model Monitoring and Maintenance:

The deployment of machine learning models is not the end of the journey. Continuously monitor model performance in production. Azure Machine Learning provides tools for tracking model behavior and data drift, and it can trigger retraining pipelines when necessary.

9. Scaling and Automation:

As your machine learning projects grow, Azure Machine Learning provides tools for scaling and automating workflows. This includes the use of machine learning pipelines for orchestrating complex processes and managing end-to-end machine learning workflows.

10. Collaboration and Versioning:

Azure Machine Learning promotes collaboration and versioning. You can work on machine learning projects with teams, and the platform helps you manage different versions of experiments, models, and datasets.

Code Illustration (Python):

Below is a simplified code example demonstrating the machine learning process using Azure Machine Learning with Python. This code covers stages from data preparation to model development and deployment.

```python
# Data preparation
# ...

# Data exploration
# ...

# Feature engineering
# ...

# Model development
# ...

# Model evaluation
```

...

Hyperparameter tuning

...

Model deployment

...

Model monitoring and maintenance

...

```

This code structure showcases the key stages of the machine learning process, from data preparation to model deployment.

Understanding and following this process is essential for successful machine learning projects. In the following sections, we'll delve into specific aspects of the machine learning process and explore topics like building predictive models with Azure Machine Learning in greater detail.

## Building Predictive Models with Azure ML

Building predictive models is a fundamental aspect of Azure Machine Learning (Azure ML). In this section, we will explore the process of creating predictive models using Azure ML, step by step.

### 1. Data Preparation:

Before you start building predictive models, you need to prepare your data. In Azure ML, you can import, clean, and preprocess data using various data manipulation tools.

### 2. Dataset Creation:
```

Azure ML allows you to create datasets from your prepared data. These datasets serve as the foundation for building your predictive models. Datasets can be tabular, text, image, or other types depending on your data.

3. Model Selection:

Choose the appropriate machine learning algorithm or model for your predictive task. Azure ML supports a wide range of models, including classification, regression, clustering, and more. You can also utilize automated machine learning (AutoML) to automatically select the best model for your data.

4. Model Training:

Train your selected model using your training dataset. Azure ML provides a user-friendly interface to define your model training process and hyperparameters. You can also monitor the training process and analyze model performance.

5. Model Evaluation:

Once your model is trained, it's essential to evaluate its performance. Azure ML offers various evaluation metrics, like accuracy, precision, recall, F1-score, and ROC curves, to assess the quality of your model.

6. Hyperparameter Tuning:

Fine-tune your model's hyperparameters to optimize its performance. Azure ML provides automated hyperparameter tuning, which helps you discover the best hyperparameter settings.

7. Model Deployment:

After selecting the best model, you can deploy it as a web service in Azure ML. This service can be used for real-time predictions in applications and services.

8. Batch Scoring:

Azure ML also allows you to perform batch scoring by submitting a batch of data to your deployed model for batch predictions. This is useful for scenarios where you have large datasets that need prediction in bulk.

9. Model Monitoring:

Continuous monitoring of your deployed model is essential to ensure it performs well over time. Azure ML provides tools for tracking and monitoring model behavior and data drift.

10. Retraining and Versioning:

If your model's performance deteriorates or your data changes significantly, you can trigger retraining pipelines in Azure ML. The platform helps you manage different versions of models and experiments.

Code Illustration (Python):

Here's a simplified code example in Python that demonstrates the process of building a predictive model using Azure ML. This code covers stages from data preparation to model evaluation and deployment:

```python
# Data preparation

# ...

# Dataset creation

# ...

# Model selection

# ...

# Model training
```

```
# ...

# Model evaluation

# ...

# Hyperparameter tuning

# ...

# Model deployment

# ...

# Batch scoring

# ...

# Model monitoring

# ...
```

This code structure provides an overview of the key steps involved in building predictive models with Azure ML. The specifics of each step will depend on your dataset and predictive task.

6.2 Building Machine Learning Models

Data Preprocessing for Machine Learning

Data preprocessing is a critical step in building effective machine learning models. In this section, we will explore the process of preparing and transforming data for machine learning using Azure Machine Learning.

1. Data Collection:

Begin by collecting your data from various sources. Azure Machine Learning supports data from databases, cloud storage, web services, and more. Import the data into your workspace.

2. Data Understanding:

Examine your data to gain insights into its characteristics. This includes checking for missing values, outliers, and understanding the data distribution. Azure ML provides tools for visualizing data and performing exploratory data analysis (EDA).

3. Data Cleaning:

Clean the data by handling missing values, duplications, and outliers. Azure ML includes modules for data cleaning and allows you to create custom data cleaning scripts.

4. Data Transformation:

Transform the data to make it suitable for machine learning. This may involve one-hot encoding categorical variables, scaling numerical features, and engineering new features. Azure ML provides a drag-and-drop interface for these transformations.

5. Feature Selection:

Select relevant features for your machine learning model. Feature selection helps reduce dimensionality and improve model performance. You can use techniques like correlation analysis and feature importance ranking.

6. Data Splitting:

Split your data into training and testing sets. The training set is used to train your model, while the testing set is used to evaluate its performance. Azure ML provides modules for data splitting and cross-validation.

7. Imbalanced Data Handling:

If your dataset is imbalanced, meaning one class is underrepresented, consider techniques like oversampling or undersampling to balance the data. Azure ML supports these techniques.

8. Data Visualization:

Visualize the preprocessed data to better understand its characteristics. You can use Azure ML for creating custom visualizations and exploring data patterns.

9. Data Export:

Once data preprocessing is complete, you can export the preprocessed dataset for model training. Azure ML allows you to save datasets in various formats.

Code Illustration (Python):

Here's a simplified code example in Python to demonstrate data preprocessing using Azure ML:

```python
```

```
# Data collection

# ...

# Data understanding

# ...

# Data cleaning

# ...

# Data transformation

# ...

# Feature selection

# ...

# Data splitting

# ...

# Imbalanced data handling

# ...

# Data visualization

# ...

# Data export

# ...
```

This code structure provides an overview of the key steps involved in data preprocessing for machine learning. The specifics of each step will depend on your dataset and the problem you're addressing.

Selecting and Training Machine Learning Models

Selecting the right machine learning model and training it is a crucial step in the data science workflow. In this section, we'll explore the process of choosing the appropriate machine learning algorithm and training it using Azure Machine Learning.

1. Model Selection:

  - Choose the appropriate machine learning algorithm for your problem. The selection depends on the nature of your data (classification, regression, clustering, etc.) and your project goals.

  - Azure Machine Learning offers a variety of built-in algorithms, including decision trees, support vector machines, neural networks, and more.

2. Feature Engineering:

  - Engineer features to represent your data effectively. This may involve creating new features, transforming existing ones, and scaling numerical attributes. Azure ML provides tools for feature engineering.

3. Model Training:

  - Split your data into training and testing sets. The training set is used to train the machine learning model. Azure ML simplifies this process with built-in modules for data splitting and cross-validation.

4. Hyperparameter Tuning:

  - Fine-tune the model's hyperparameters to improve its performance. This can be done manually or automatically using techniques like grid search or random search.

5. Model Training and Evaluation:

- Train the machine learning model on the training data using Azure ML's training modules.

- Evaluate the model's performance on the testing data. Common evaluation metrics include accuracy, precision, recall, and F1 score for classification tasks, or mean squared error and R-squared for regression tasks.

6. Model Comparison:

- Compare the performance of different models if you've tried multiple algorithms. Azure ML provides tools for model comparison and tracking.

7. Model Interpretation:

- Interpret the trained model to understand the impact of different features on predictions. This is especially important for decision-making processes.

8. Model Export:

- Once you're satisfied with the model's performance, export it for deployment. Azure ML allows you to save models in various formats, including ONNX and Docker containers.

Code Illustration (Python):

Here's a simplified Python code example to demonstrate selecting and training a machine learning model using Azure ML:

```python
from azureml.train import automl

# Load data
# ...
```

```
# Define AutoML configuration

automl_config    =    AutoMLConfig(task='classification',    primary_metric='accuracy',
max_time_in_minutes=30, iterations=5)

# Run AutoML

run = experiment.submit(automl_config)

# Retrieve the best model

best_run, fitted_model = run.get_output()

# ...

# Export the model

fitted_model.save(model_name='best_model',
model_framework=Model.Framework.SCIKITLEARN, model_framework_version='0.22.2')
```

In this code, we used Azure AutoML to automatically select and train the best model for a classification task. The process can be adapted for different machine learning problems.

Please note that this is a simplified example, and the specific steps may vary depending on your project.

Model Evaluation and Deployment

After selecting, training, and fine-tuning your machine learning model, the next crucial steps are model evaluation and deployment. In this section, we will delve into the process of assessing your model's performance and making it available for production use.

1. Model Evaluation:

- Before deploying a machine learning model, you must evaluate its performance thoroughly. This step involves various metrics depending on the type of problem, such as accuracy, precision, recall, F1 score for classification, or mean squared error, and R-squared for regression. Azure Machine Learning offers built-in tools to calculate these metrics.

2. Model Interpretability:

- Understand the model's decisions by interpreting it. This helps in building trust and ensuring that the model's predictions align with the expected behavior.

3. Model Deployment:

- Once you are satisfied with your model's performance, it's time to deploy it to make predictions in real-time or batch mode. Azure ML provides multiple deployment options, including Azure Kubernetes Service (AKS), Azure Container Instances (ACI), and more.

4. Endpoint Configuration:

- Set up the deployment configuration, specifying factors like scalability, authentication, and monitoring. Azure ML facilitates endpoint configuration with customizable settings.

5. Testing Deployed Model:

- After deploying the model, it's essential to thoroughly test it to ensure it works as expected. Test it with different input data to identify any potential issues.

6. Monitoring and Logging:

- Continuous monitoring of the deployed model is vital. Azure ML offers monitoring solutions to keep track of the model's performance and detect anomalies or deviations.

7. A/B Testing:

- Consider running A/B tests to compare the deployed model's performance with its predecessor or other models. This helps make data-driven decisions regarding model updates.

8. Model Versioning:

- Keep track of different versions of your models for rollback or model management. Azure ML provides model versioning capabilities.

9. Scalability:

- Ensure the deployed model can handle varying workloads and demand. Azure ML allows you to scale resources based on usage patterns.

10. Security and Compliance:

- Implement security measures to protect your model and the data it processes. Ensure compliance with relevant regulations and standards.

11. Real-time and Batch Scoring:

- Deploy your model to perform real-time scoring, allowing it to make predictions instantly. Additionally, you can set up batch scoring for processing large datasets efficiently.

Code Illustration (Azure ML Service):

Below is an example of deploying a machine learning model using Azure Machine Learning Service:

```python
from azureml.core import Workspace, Model
```

```python
from azureml.core.webservice import AksWebservice, Webservice
from azureml.core.model import InferenceConfig

# Load the Azure ML workspace
ws = Workspace.from_config()

# Retrieve the model to deploy
model = Model(workspace=ws, name='my-model')

# Define inference configuration
inference_config = InferenceConfig(entry_script='score.py', environment=myenv)

# Deploy the model as a web service on AKS
aks_config = AksWebservice.deploy_configuration(cpu_cores=1, memory_gb=1)
aks_service = Model.deploy(workspace=ws,
            name='my-aks-service',
            models=[model],
            inference_config=inference_config,
            deployment_config=aks_config)
aks_service.wait_for_deployment(show_output=True)
```

This code demonstrates deploying a model as a web service on Azure Kubernetes Service (AKS). It involves configuring the inference environment, deployment, and monitoring the deployment process.

6.3 Integration with Power BI for Predictive Analytics

Embedding Machine Learning Models in Power BI

Embedding machine learning models in Power BI reports allows you to create predictive analytics dashboards that provide real-time insights and recommendations. In this section, we will explore how to integrate Azure Machine Learning models into Power BI for enhanced data visualization.

1. Model Creation and Deployment:

- Start by creating and deploying your machine learning model using Azure Machine Learning service, as discussed in the previous chapters.

2. Model Endpoint:

- Your deployed model should have an endpoint that allows real-time scoring. This endpoint can be used to make predictions based on input data.

3. Power BI Desktop:

- Ensure you have Power BI Desktop installed, as this is the tool for creating your reports and dashboards.

4. Power Query Editor:

- Power BI provides Power Query Editor, which you can use to connect to various data sources, including your Azure Machine Learning model's endpoint.

5. Data Source Connection:

- In Power BI, create a connection to your model's endpoint using Power Query. You will need to define the HTTP request to send to your model and how to handle the response.

6. Real-time Predictions:

- Use Power Query to send real-time data to your machine learning model. Configure the refresh rate for your data source so that it periodically fetches new data and updates predictions.

7. Data Visualization:

- Create visualizations in Power BI reports based on the predictions from your machine learning model. You can use these visualizations to display recommendations, forecasts, or insights.

8. Real-time Updates:

- Power BI can provide real-time updates, ensuring that your reports are always displaying the latest predictions from your machine learning model.

9. Interactive Dashboards:

- Design interactive dashboards that allow users to explore data and predictions. Use slicers, filters, and bookmarks to make the reports user-friendly.

10. Monitoring and Maintenance:

- Regularly monitor your Power BI reports to ensure that the machine learning model is working correctly. If needed, update the model and the report accordingly.

Code Illustration:

Here's a high-level example of embedding an Azure Machine Learning model into Power BI for real-time predictions. The exact steps will depend on your model and its deployment.

```powerquery
let

    source = Json.Document(Web.Contents("YOUR_MODEL_ENDPOINT",
[Content=Text.ToBinary("YOUR_JSON_REQUEST")])),


    // Extract the prediction from the response

    prediction = source[prediction]

in

    prediction
```

In this code snippet, we use Power Query in Power BI to make an HTTP request to the model's endpoint and extract the prediction from the response.

Real-time Predictive Analytics in Power BI Reports

Incorporating real-time predictive analytics into your Power BI reports allows for dynamic, data-driven decision-making. This section will guide you through the process of creating Power BI reports that provide real-time insights and recommendations based on embedded Azure Machine Learning models.

1. Model Deployment:

- First, make sure your machine learning model is deployed and has a real-time scoring endpoint as discussed in the previous chapters.

2. Power BI Desktop:

- Launch Power BI Desktop to begin building your reports. This tool allows you to create visually appealing dashboards with real-time analytics.

3. Data Connection:

- Connect your Power BI report to your model's real-time scoring endpoint using Power Query. This connection enables Power BI to send data to the model and receive real-time predictions.

4. Streaming Data:

- Set up data streaming in Power BI so that it continuously collects and sends data to the model for predictions. You can configure the refresh rate to match your real-time requirements.

5. Visualization Components:

- Create visualizations within your Power BI reports to showcase the predictions from your machine learning model. This can include charts, tables, and custom visuals.

6. Dynamic Dashboards:

- Design interactive and dynamic dashboards that respond to real-time data. Use filters, slicers, bookmarks, and drill-through features to provide users with an immersive experience.

7. Real-time Refresh:

- Power BI can be configured to refresh data at specified intervals. Set up automatic refresh to ensure your reports are always showing the latest predictions.

8. Alerts and Notifications:

- Implement alerts and notifications in Power BI to notify users when specific conditions or predictions are met. This can be done using Power Automate or other notification mechanisms.

9. User Interaction:

- Consider the user experience when designing your reports. Make it easy for users to interact with the data and understand the insights provided by your embedded machine learning model.

10. Mobile Optimization:

- Ensure that your real-time predictive analytics reports are optimized for mobile devices. Power BI offers mobile layout options for a seamless experience on smartphones and tablets.

11. Continuous Monitoring:

- Regularly monitor the performance of your Power BI reports and the underlying machine learning model. Make adjustments as needed based on feedback and data quality.

Sample Code:

Here's a simplified example of how to create a real-time connection to your Azure Machine Learning model within Power BI. The exact implementation will depend on your specific model and data.

```powerbi
let
```

```
realTimeData = Table.FromList({Text.From(DateTime.LocalNow())},
Splitter.SplitByNothing()),

realTimePrediction = Table.AddColumn(realTimeData, "Prediction", each
YourMachineLearningModel(realTimeData)),

predictionValue = realTimePrediction{0}[Prediction]

in

    predictionValue
```

In this example, we use Power Query to create a real-time data source and obtain predictions from your machine learning model.

Monitoring and Managing Azure Machine Learning Models in Power BI

Monitoring and managing your Azure Machine Learning models within Power BI is crucial to ensure their performance and reliability. This section will guide you through the steps for overseeing and maintaining your models effectively.

1. Model Lifecycle:

   - Understand the lifecycle of your machine learning models. This includes model development, training, deployment, and retraining. Plan for regular model updates to keep your predictions accurate.

2. Azure Machine Learning Service:

   - Utilize Azure Machine Learning Service to centralize model management. This platform enables you to organize your models, track their performance, and automate tasks like retraining.

3. Model Versioning:

- Implement version control for your machine learning models. Versioning allows you to track changes and easily revert to a previous model version if needed.

4. Performance Metrics:

- Define and measure performance metrics for your models. These metrics could include accuracy, precision, recall, and others relevant to your specific use case.

5. Logging and Monitoring:

- Set up logging and monitoring for your deployed models. Azure provides various tools for monitoring model endpoints, such as Azure Monitor, Application Insights, and Log Analytics.

6. Alerting System:

- Configure alerts for model performance issues or anomalies. Azure Monitor and Application Insights can trigger alerts based on predefined criteria.

7. Retraining Strategy:

- Determine the retraining strategy for your models. This may involve setting a schedule or triggering retraining based on data drift or model degradation.

8. Data Drift Detection:

- Implement data drift detection to identify when the data distribution used for model training significantly differs from real-time data. This can be done using Azure Machine Learning's data drift monitoring.

9. Reporting in Power BI:

- Create Power BI reports that provide insights into model performance. Visualize metrics, anomalies, and other relevant data to monitor your machine learning models.

10. Automation:

- Automate tasks like model retraining and version deployment using Azure Machine Learning pipelines and Power Automate to streamline your workflow.

Sample Code:

The following code is a simplified example of how you can monitor and manage your Azure Machine Learning models using Azure Monitor and Application Insights in Power BI.

```powerbi
let
    metricsData = AzureMonitor.GetMetric(Namespace, MetricName, [IntervalStart =
DateTime.From(DateTime.Add(DateTime.LocalNow(), -1)), IntervalEnd =
DateTime.LocalNow()]),

    performanceMetric = Table.AddColumn(metricsData, "Performance Metric", each
YourMetricCalculationFunction(metricsData))
in
    performanceMetric
```

In this code, we retrieve metrics data from Azure Monitor, calculate relevant performance metrics, and visualize them in Power BI.

CHAPTER VI
Scalable Solutions with Azure and Power BI

7.1 Designing Scalable Architectures

Scalability Challenges and Solutions

Scalability is a crucial aspect of designing solutions with Azure and Power BI. Ensuring that your architecture can handle growing data and user demands is essential. In this section, we'll explore the challenges and solutions related to scalability.

Scalability Challenges:

1. Data Volume: As your organization accumulates more data, it can become challenging to process, store, and analyze large datasets efficiently.

2. Performance: Increasing data volume can lead to performance bottlenecks, resulting in slow query response times in Power BI reports.

3. Concurrent Users: Handling multiple users accessing Power BI reports simultaneously requires a scalable architecture to prevent system overload.

4. Real-time Data: Integrating real-time data streams into your solution can strain resources and affect performance.

Scalability Solutions:

1. Azure Data Lake Storage and Azure SQL Data Warehouse: Use Azure's scalable data storage and processing solutions to handle large datasets. Data Lake Storage Gen2 provides a unified data repository, and Azure SQL Data Warehouse can scale resources on-demand for data warehousing needs.

2. Power BI Premium: Consider using Power BI Premium or Premium Per User (PPU) for scalability. Premium offers dedicated capacity and enhanced performance, suitable for handling larger datasets and concurrent users.

3. Azure Analysis Services: Deploy your Power BI data models to Azure Analysis Services for better performance and scalability. This allows you to offload data processing from Power BI Desktop to a dedicated service.

4. Azure Stream Analytics: When dealing with real-time data, use Azure Stream Analytics to ingest, process, and push data to Power BI for real-time analytics. Stream Analytics can scale to accommodate data streaming demands.

5. Auto-scaling: Implement auto-scaling for your Azure resources. Azure provides tools like Azure Functions and Logic Apps for automated scaling based on triggers such as high resource utilization or increased user load.

6. Data Partitioning: Divide large datasets into partitions, and apply techniques like data compression and columnstore indexes to enhance query performance.

Sample Code:

Here's a simplified example of how you can use Azure Functions to trigger auto-scaling based on resource utilization:

```csharp
using System;

using Microsoft.Azure.WebJobs;

using Microsoft.Extensions.Logging;

public static class AutoScalingFunction
{
    [FunctionName("MonitorResourceUtilization")]
    public static void Run(
        [TimerTrigger("0 */5 * * * *")] TimerInfo myTimer,
        ILogger log)
    {
        // Check resource utilization and trigger scaling actions if needed.
        // Implement your scaling logic here.
        log.LogInformation($"C# Timer trigger function executed at: {DateTime.Now}");
    }
}
```

In this code, an Azure Function is scheduled to run at five-minute intervals to monitor resource utilization. When thresholds are exceeded, it can trigger scaling actions to ensure scalability.

Architectural Considerations for Scalable Solutions

When designing scalable architectures for Azure and Power BI, there are several critical considerations you should take into account. These architectural considerations will help you ensure that your solution can efficiently handle growing data volumes, user demands, and real-time data streaming. Here are the key aspects to focus on:

1. Data Storage and Management:

- **Azure Data Lake Storage and Azure SQL Data Warehouse:** Leverage Azure Data Lake Storage Gen2 for scalable, secure data storage. Consider using Azure SQL Data Warehouse for advanced analytics and data warehousing. Ensure that data is organized effectively for optimized query performance.

2. Data Processing and Transformation:

- **Data Transformation Pipelines:** Design efficient data transformation pipelines using tools like Azure Data Factory, Azure Databricks, or Power Query in Power BI. Implement data processing that minimizes resource consumption and maximizes scalability.

3. Data Modeling and Reporting:

- **Azure Analysis Services:** Offload data modeling and processing to Azure Analysis Services for enhanced performance. Use aggregations and caching for faster query responses in Power BI reports.

- **Power BI Premium:** Consider using Power BI Premium or Premium Per User (PPU) to take advantage of dedicated capacity and scalability for both data modeling and report rendering.

4. Real-time Data Streams:

- Azure Stream Analytics: For real-time data streaming, design Azure Stream Analytics jobs to ingest, process, and push data to Power BI. Configure Stream Analytics for scalability based on data volume and velocity.

5. Scalability and Load Balancing:

- Auto-scaling: Implement auto-scaling mechanisms for Azure resources to adapt to varying workloads. Azure Functions, Logic Apps, and Virtual Machine Scale Sets can help automate resource scaling.

- Load Balancing: Use Azure Load Balancers or Application Gateways to distribute traffic evenly across multiple instances, ensuring high availability and scalability.

6. Security and Compliance:

- Azure Security Center: Implement robust security measures using Azure Security Center to protect your data and resources. Ensure compliance with regulatory standards.

7. Monitoring and Alerting:

- Azure Monitor and Azure Application Insights: Set up comprehensive monitoring and alerting solutions to track resource utilization, application performance, and user interactions. Configure alerts to respond to scalability issues promptly.

Sample Code (Monitoring and Alerting):

Here's a simple example of setting up an alert in Azure Monitor using Azure Resource Manager templates:

```json
{
```

```json
    "$schema": "https://schema.management.azure.com/schemas/2019-04-01/deploymentTemplate.json#",
    "contentVersion": "1.0.0.0",
    "resources": [
        {
            "type": "Microsoft.Insights/metricAlerts",
            "apiVersion": "2018-03-01",
            "name": "ResourceAlert",
            "location": "global",
            "tags": {},
            "properties": {
                "description": "Alert for high CPU utilization",
                "severity": 3,
                "enabled": true,
                "scopes": [],
                "evaluationFrequency": "PT1M",
                "windowSize": "PT5M",
                "criteria": {
                    "odata.type": "Microsoft.Azure.Monitor.SingleResourceMultipleMetricCriteria",
                    "allOf": [
                        {
                            "name": "metricName",
                            "operator": "Equals",
                            "value": "Percentage CPU"
                        },
```

```json
                {
                    "name": "aggregationType",
                    "operator": "Equals",
                    "value": "Average"
                },
                {
                    "name": "threshold",
                    "operator": "GreaterThan",
                    "value": 80
                }
            ]
        },
        "actions": []
    }
  }
]
}
```

This JSON template creates an alert to monitor CPU utilization and trigger an action when it exceeds 80%. The actual alert action would depend on your chosen response, such as scaling Azure resources.

These architectural considerations and the sample code will help you design a scalable solution that efficiently utilizes Azure and Power BI resources to meet your organization's needs.

Scaling Power BI and Azure Resources

Scalability is a crucial aspect of designing architectures that can handle increased workloads and data volumes efficiently. Scaling Power BI and Azure resources involves the strategic allocation of computing power, memory, and storage resources to meet performance and capacity demands. Below, we'll explore how to scale both Power BI and Azure resources.

1. Scaling Power BI:

- **Power BI Premium:** Power BI Premium and Power BI Premium Per User (PPU) are dedicated capacities that allow you to allocate more resources to your Power BI workspaces. This is essential for handling larger datasets, complex data models, and more concurrent users.

- **Auto-scaling:** Power BI Premium Gen2 supports auto-scaling. You can configure workspaces to automatically add or remove capacity based on the number of active users. This helps manage resources efficiently.

- **Power BI Embedded:** For embedding Power BI reports in applications, you can consider Power BI Embedded. This service allows for scaling capacity based on usage.

2. Scaling Azure Resources:

- **Virtual Machine Scaling:** Azure provides Virtual Machine Scale Sets that allow you to automatically adjust the number of VM instances based on demand. Configure scaling rules to add or remove VMs as necessary.

- **Azure Functions:** Serverless Azure Functions can auto-scale to handle varying workloads. These are useful for implementing event-driven architectures without manual intervention.

- Azure Kubernetes Service (AKS): For containerized applications, AKS allows for horizontal scaling of containers to distribute workloads effectively.

- Azure Logic Apps: Use Logic Apps to automate workflows and processes in response to events. Logic Apps can be configured to scale dynamically.

- Azure App Service: For web applications, Azure App Service provides auto-scaling capabilities to manage web server instances based on traffic.

3. Setting Up Auto-scaling (Azure VMs):

To set up auto-scaling for Azure VMs, you can use Azure Virtual Machine Scale Sets. Here's an example of how to configure auto-scaling using Azure PowerShell:

1. Create a scale set with a specific image and instance count:

```powershell
$vmss = New-AzVmss -ResourceGroupName "MyResourceGroup" -Location "East US" -VMScaleSetName "MyVMSS" -VirtualNetworkName "MyVNET" -InstanceCount 2
```

2. Define auto-scaling rules, such as CPU percentage:

```powershell
Add-AzVmssAutoScaleRule -ResourceGroupName "MyResourceGroup" -VMScaleSetName "MyVMSS" -ScaleIn -NumberOfInstances 1 -MetricName "Percentage CPU" -Operator "GreaterThan" -Threshold 70 -Direction "Decrease" -ChangeCount 1
```

```
Add-AzVmssAutoScaleRule -ResourceGroupName "MyResourceGroup" -VMScaleSetName
"MyVMSS" -ScaleOut -NumberOfInstances 1 -MetricName "Percentage CPU" -Operator
"LessThan" -Threshold 30 -Direction "Increase" -ChangeCount 1
```

```
```

3. Set up the application within the VMs to automatically handle the scaling events.

By implementing auto-scaling for Azure resources and utilizing the scaling options available in Power BI, you can ensure that your architecture efficiently adapts to the needs of your growing user base and data volumes. This is a critical aspect of designing scalable solutions with Azure and Power BI.

7.2 Performance Optimization and Best Practices

Optimizing Data Processing in Azure

Optimizing data processing in Azure is essential for ensuring that your data workflows are efficient, cost-effective, and capable of handling large volumes of data. Here are some strategies and best practices for optimizing data processing in Azure:

1. Data Pipeline Architecture:

- Design a well-architected data pipeline that considers factors like data ingestion, transformation, and storage. Azure offers services like Azure Data Factory, Azure Logic Apps, and Azure Functions for building data pipelines.

2. Azure Data Lake Storage Gen2:

- Utilize Azure Data Lake Storage Gen2 for storing large volumes of data. It provides features like hierarchical namespace, scalability, and integration with various Azure services.

3. Azure Data Factory:

- Azure Data Factory is a fully managed data integration service that allows you to create data-driven workflows. Optimize your data processing pipelines in Azure Data Factory for efficiency.

4. Data Compression:

- Compress data files to reduce storage and data transfer costs. Azure supports various compression formats like GZIP, BZIP2, and Snappy.

5. Parallel Processing:

- Leverage the parallel processing capabilities of services like Azure Databricks or Azure HDInsight to distribute data processing tasks across multiple nodes, improving performance.

6. Monitoring and Scaling:

- Implement monitoring solutions to keep track of resource utilization. Use Azure Monitor, Log Analytics, and Azure Application Insights to gain insights into the performance of your data processing workflows.

7. Data Partitioning:

- Partition large datasets in a way that aligns with your query patterns. Azure services like Azure SQL Data Warehouse and Cosmos DB support data partitioning for improved query performance.

8. Data Caching:

- Utilize Azure Cache for Redis or Azure SQL Database's caching features to reduce the need for repetitive data processing.

9. Data Quality:

- Ensure data quality by implementing data validation and cleansing routines in your processing workflows. Services like Azure Data Factory and Azure Databricks offer tools for data preparation and transformation.

10. Serverless Computing:

- Consider using serverless Azure Functions for lightweight data processing tasks. These functions automatically scale based on demand, reducing costs.

11. Data Retention Policies:

- Define data retention policies to manage the lifecycle of your data. Azure Blob Storage provides features for setting data retention rules.

12. Cost Management:

- Regularly review and optimize your data processing costs. Use Azure Cost Management and Billing to analyze spending and identify cost-saving opportunities.

13. Distributed Processing:

- Implement distributed data processing techniques for tasks like large-scale data transformations. Services like Azure HDInsight with Apache Spark are suitable for such tasks.

14. Data Encryption:

- Encrypt data at rest and in transit using Azure's encryption capabilities to ensure data security.

Optimizing data processing in Azure requires a combination of efficient architecture, choice of the right Azure services, monitoring, and continuous improvement. By following these best practices, you can ensure that your data processing workflows are well-tuned for performance and cost-effectiveness.

Designing Efficient Data Models in Power BI

Efficient data modeling is crucial for creating high-performance Power BI reports and dashboards. Proper data modeling ensures that your reports respond quickly and provide an excellent user experience. Here are the key steps and best practices for designing efficient data models in Power BI:

1. Data Source Selection:

- Choose the right data sources that are well-structured and optimized for reporting. Ensure data sources are designed with the reporting needs in mind.

2. Data Import vs. DirectQuery:

- Understand the trade-offs between importing data into Power BI and using DirectQuery. Importing data provides better performance for most scenarios, but DirectQuery may be necessary for large datasets or real-time data.

3. Data Transformation:

- Use Power Query Editor to transform and clean data before importing it into Power BI. Eliminate unnecessary columns, handle missing data, and create calculated columns as needed.

4. Data Modeling Best Practices:

- Follow star schema or snowflake schema design patterns. These patterns help organize data into fact tables and dimension tables, optimizing query performance.

5. Relationships:

- Define relationships between tables. Use one-to-many or many-to-one relationships for connecting fact and dimension tables. Avoid creating circular or ambiguous relationships.

6. DAX Optimization:

- Write efficient Data Analysis Expressions (DAX) measures. Avoid using complex DAX calculations that might slow down query performance. Optimize DAX formulas for better responsiveness.

7. Use Hierarchies:

- Create hierarchies for fields like date, time, or location. Hierarchies allow for easy drill-down in reports and improve user navigation.

8. Aggregations:

- Create aggregations on large datasets to speed up query performance. Aggregations store pre-summarized data to respond faster to user queries.

9. Use Composite Models:

- Leverage composite models, which allow combining DirectQuery and imported data in a single report. This can be useful for large datasets where real-time data is needed.

10. Reduce Cardinality:

- Reduce the cardinality of columns with high distinct values. High cardinality columns can slow down query performance. Consider grouping or categorizing data to reduce distinct values.

11. Sorting and Filtering:

- Define the default sorting and filtering behaviors in your data model. This can help improve the user experience by presenting data in a meaningful way.

12. Testing and Optimization:

- Regularly test your data models with large datasets and complex reports. Identify and resolve performance bottlenecks as they arise.

13. Query Folding:

- Ensure that as much of the data transformation is performed in the source database as possible. Power BI's query folding feature pushes transformations back to the data source, improving performance.

14. Use the Performance Analyzer:

- The Power BI Performance Analyzer tool helps identify performance bottlenecks in your reports. Use it to pinpoint areas that need improvement.

15. Refresh Schedule:

- Set an appropriate data refresh schedule to keep your reports up to date without overloading your data sources.

By following these best practices, you can create efficient data models in Power BI that provide fast response times, enabling users to interact with reports and dashboards seamlessly. It's essential to continually monitor and optimize your data models as your data and reporting requirements evolve.

Monitoring and Tuning for Performance

Monitoring and tuning are essential aspects of maintaining a high-performance Power BI solution. By continuously tracking your system's performance and making necessary adjustments, you can ensure your reports and dashboards deliver optimal user experiences. Here's a comprehensive guide on monitoring and tuning for performance in Power BI:

1. Performance Analysis in Power BI:

- Use built-in Power BI tools like Performance Analyzer and Query Diagnostics to analyze report and query performance. These tools help identify bottlenecks in your reports and queries.

2. User Feedback:

- Collect feedback from end-users regarding the performance of reports. Their insights can reveal issues that might not be apparent during your own testing.

3. Data Refresh Monitoring:

- Keep an eye on data refresh times. If data sources change or expand, the data refresh process might need adjustment to accommodate the new data.

4. Query Performance Tuning:

- Optimize your DAX queries and data models. Focus on slow-performing queries and apply DAX optimizations to improve report response times.

5. Data Source Optimization:

- Ensure data sources are properly indexed and optimized. This is particularly important for DirectQuery or Live Connection scenarios.

6. Query Folding:

- Leverage query folding to push data transformations back to the data source, reducing data transfer and improving query performance.

7. Data Compression:

- Check data compression settings in Power BI. Proper data compression can significantly improve report performance.

8. Data Model Size:

- Monitor the size of your data model. Smaller data models tend to perform better, so remove unnecessary data and columns.

9. Scheduled Data Refresh:

- Schedule data refresh during off-peak hours to minimize impact on report performance.

10. Indexing:

- If using DirectQuery or Live Connection, ensure the underlying database tables are appropriately indexed. Well-indexed databases can significantly improve query performance.

11. Partitioning:

- Use table partitioning for large datasets. Partitioning helps to segment data into smaller, manageable chunks, which can improve query performance.

12. Review the Query Execution Plan:

- Understand the query execution plan in Power BI. Review it to identify areas where optimization is needed.

13. Evaluate Gateway Performance:

- If using a gateway for on-premises data sources, monitor the gateway's performance and resource utilization.

14. Regular Testing:

- Continuously test your reports and dashboards with representative data volumes and user interaction scenarios. This ensures you catch performance issues early.

15. Regular Updates:

- Keep your Power BI desktop application and the Power BI service updated to leverage the latest performance improvements and features.

16. Resource Scaling:

- For Azure-hosted Power BI services, consider scaling resources up or down based on usage. This can ensure adequate resources are available during peak usage.

17. Advanced Analysis Tools:

- Consider using external performance analysis tools and utilities to gain deeper insights into query and report performance.

18. Documentation:

- Maintain documentation of performance-related issues, their solutions, and best practices. Share this information with your team for reference.

19. User Training:

- Train end-users on best practices for report interaction and filtering to help them make efficient use of reports.

By diligently monitoring and tuning your Power BI solution for performance, you can maintain a responsive and efficient reporting environment for your organization. Regularly revisit and adjust these optimization techniques as your data and reporting needs evolve.

7.3 Monitoring and Scaling Resources

Azure Resource Monitoring and Alerts

In the context of maintaining a scalable and well-performing Power BI solution, monitoring Azure resources is crucial. This section will guide you on how to effectively monitor Azure resources and set up alerts to stay informed about their status.

1. Azure Monitor:

- Azure Monitor is a comprehensive service that provides a unified solution for collecting, analyzing, and acting on telemetry from your Azure environment. Begin by navigating to Azure Monitor in the Azure portal.

2. Monitoring Dashboards:

- Azure Monitor allows you to create custom monitoring dashboards. Set up a dashboard that includes the key metrics and resources relevant to your Power BI solution.

3. Metrics and Logs:

- Use Azure Monitor to access metrics and logs for Azure resources related to your Power BI deployment. These metrics can include CPU usage, memory, data transfer, and more.

4. Metrics Alerts:

- Set up metrics-based alerts to be notified when resource metrics exceed predefined thresholds. For example, create alerts for high CPU usage or low memory availability.

5. Log Alerts:

- Utilize log alerts to detect specific events or issues within your Azure resources. You can define log queries to identify and alert on specific log events.

6. Activity Logs:

- Monitor Azure Activity Logs to track events that impact your resources. Be especially vigilant for activities that might affect Power BI workspaces or data sources.

7. Alert Rules:

- Define alert rules to specify the conditions under which you want to be notified. For example, set an alert to trigger when a particular Azure resource becomes unavailable.

8. Alert Notification Channels:

- Configure the channels through which you wish to receive alerts. Azure supports various channels, such as email, SMS, and webhook notifications.

9. Scheduled Reports:

- Azure Monitor allows you to schedule and receive detailed reports about the state and performance of your resources. Consider scheduling regular reports to stay informed.

10. Resource Dependencies:

- Keep an eye on resource dependencies. If your Power BI solution relies on other Azure services, monitor them to ensure they don't become bottlenecks.

11. Fine-Tuning Alerts:

- Regularly review your alerts to ensure they are correctly configured. Adjust alert thresholds as needed to prevent unnecessary notifications.

12. Integration with Azure Logic Apps:

- Use Azure Logic Apps to create customized workflows for alert notifications and automated responses to specific events.

13. Historical Analysis:

- Analyze historical metrics and logs to identify patterns and trends that can help you proactively address performance and scalability challenges.

14. Cost Management:

- Consider cost management tools to track and control Azure spending, especially as it relates to Power BI workspaces and capacities.

15. Resource Recommendations:

- Leverage Azure Advisor to receive recommendations for optimizing your Azure resources based on best practices.

Effective monitoring and alerting can help you address issues before they affect the performance of your Power BI solution. By keeping a close watch on Azure resources and setting up alerts, you can maintain a responsive and scalable environment for your organization.

Autoscaling in Azure

Autoscaling in Azure is a crucial feature for ensuring that your resources can handle variable workloads efficiently. When dealing with Power BI workspaces and associated resources, autoscaling can help you automatically adjust the capacity to meet demand. Here's a comprehensive guide on how to set up autoscaling in Azure:

1. Identify the Need for Autoscaling:

- Before implementing autoscaling, you need to identify which Azure resources or services require it. For Power BI, workspaces and data sources can benefit from autoscaling based on varying workloads and user demand.

2. Azure Autoscale Service:

- Azure offers the Azure Autoscale service to manage the autoscaling of different resources. You can access this service through the Azure portal.

3. Scaling Criteria:

- Define the criteria under which you want to scale your resources. For Power BI workspaces, you might want to consider metrics such as CPU utilization, memory usage, or the number of concurrent users.

4. Autoscale Rules:

- Create autoscale rules based on the scaling criteria. These rules define what actions should be taken when certain conditions are met. For example, you can specify that if CPU usage exceeds a certain threshold for a specified time, additional resources should be allocated.

5. Scale In and Out:

- Determine how your resources should scale. For instance, autoscaling can be set to scale out by adding more resources when demand increases or to scale in by removing resources when demand decreases.

6. Target Resource:

- Define the specific Azure resource you want to scale. In the context of Power BI, this could be a workspace or the underlying Azure services used by Power BI, such as Azure SQL Data Warehouse or Azure Data Lake Storage.

7. Alert and Notification Settings:

- Configure alerts and notifications to stay informed about autoscaling actions. Azure allows you to set up notifications through email, SMS, or webhooks.

8. Resource-Specific Considerations:

- Keep in mind that different resources may have unique autoscaling configurations. Power BI workspaces may scale differently compared to Azure SQL Data Warehouse or virtual machines. Be sure to understand the specifics of each resource's autoscale capabilities.

9. Testing and Validation:

- Before deploying autoscaling in a production environment, thoroughly test and validate your autoscaling rules and configurations. Ensure that the scaling actions are appropriate for your specific workload.

10. Monitoring and Fine-Tuning:

- Continuously monitor your autoscaling solution to make adjustments as necessary. Metrics and logs provided by Azure can help you fine-tune your autoscaling rules for optimal performance.

11. Cost Management:

- Keep an eye on the costs associated with autoscaling. Autoscaling can increase resource usage and cost. Implement cost management tools and policies to maintain control over your spending.

12. Integration with Azure Logic Apps:

- Consider using Azure Logic Apps to create customized workflows that respond to autoscaling events, such as sending notifications to administrators or running specific scripts.

13. Documentation and Best Practices:

- Document your autoscaling configurations, and follow Azure's best practices to ensure a successful autoscaling implementation.

Autoscaling in Azure can greatly enhance the performance and efficiency of your Power BI workspaces and associated resources. By automating resource allocation based on demand, you can ensure that your users have a responsive and scalable environment, even during peak usage periods.

Scaling Power BI Workspaces and Capacities

Scaling Power BI workspaces and capacities is essential to ensure that your Power BI environment can handle growing data, users, and workloads. In this section, we'll discuss the steps to effectively scale your Power BI resources:

1. Assess Current Workload:

- Before making any scaling decisions, it's crucial to assess your current workload. Understand the data volume, user concurrency, and performance bottlenecks in your Power BI workspaces.

2. Utilize Power BI Premium:

- Power BI Premium offers dedicated resources for your organization. If you're not already on Power BI Premium, consider upgrading. It provides features like increased dataset sizes, paginated reports, and advanced security settings.

3. Dedicated Capacity:

- Allocate dedicated capacities within Power BI Premium. This allows you to manage resource allocation more effectively.

4. Manage Workspaces:

- Group reports, dashboards, and datasets into logical workspaces. Consider workspaces for specific teams or departments. This segmentation can help you manage resource allocation more efficiently.

5. Resource Metrics:

- Monitor resource metrics, such as memory and CPU utilization, for each workspace. Power BI provides these metrics in the admin portal.

6. Scale Workspaces Individually:

- Not all workspaces will have the same resource requirements. You can scale workspaces individually based on their specific needs. For example, allocate more resources to workspaces with high data refresh rates or complex reports.

7. Adjust Capacity Allocation:

- Review capacity allocation regularly. If you observe resource bottlenecks or slow performance, consider adjusting the capacity allocation for individual workspaces.

8. Dataset Optimization:

- Optimize your datasets. Reducing unnecessary data, aggregating data, and implementing effective data models can significantly improve performance and reduce resource usage.

9. Paginated Reports:

- If your organization relies on paginated reports, consider offloading this workload to a dedicated capacity to avoid impacting other Power BI workspaces.

10. Data Refresh Optimization:

- Optimize data refresh schedules to spread out the workload and prevent data refresh bottlenecks during peak usage times.

11. Monitor User Activity:

- Monitor user activity and identify which reports or dashboards receive the most attention. Allocate resources accordingly to ensure optimal performance for critical content.

12. Resource Allocation Rules:

- Define resource allocation rules based on the workspace's priority and importance. This can include setting maximum and minimum resource limits.

13. Performance Testing:

- Perform performance testing to ensure that resource allocation adjustments have the desired impact on report and dashboard performance.

14. Collaborate with Users:

- Collaborate with workspace owners and report creators to understand their resource requirements and make informed decisions about capacity allocation.

15. Regular Review:

- Regularly review the allocated resources and adjust them as necessary to meet changing demands.

16. Cost Considerations:

- Be mindful of the cost implications of resource allocation. Balancing performance and cost is essential.

17. Implement Monitoring and Alerts:

- Implement monitoring and alerts for critical workspaces to detect issues early and take action proactively.

18. Documentation:

- Document your resource allocation rules and the reasoning behind them. This documentation can help in decision-making and resource management.

Scaling Power BI workspaces and capacities involves a combination of understanding your specific workload, effective resource allocation, and continuous monitoring. By following these steps and considering the unique needs of your organization, you can ensure that your Power BI environment remains performant as it scales to meet growing demands.

CHAPTER VII
Security and Compliance

8.1 Data Security in the Cloud

Cloud Data Security Challenges

As organizations transition to cloud-based solutions, they face several data security challenges that are unique to cloud environments. Understanding these challenges is crucial for implementing robust data security practices. In this section, we'll explore some of the common cloud data security challenges and how to address them.

1. Data Breaches:

   - **Challenge:** Storing data in the cloud exposes it to potential data breaches. Unauthorized access or cyberattacks can lead to data leaks.

   - **Solution:** Implement strong access controls, encryption, and monitoring. Use Azure's built-in security features to protect your data.

2. Identity and Access Management:

   - **Challenge:** Managing identities and access to cloud resources can be complex, leading to potential security gaps.

   - **Solution:** Use Azure Active Directory for centralized identity management. Implement role-based access control (RBAC) to control who can access what resources.

3. Data Encryption:

- **Challenge:** Protecting data at rest and in transit is crucial. Inadequate encryption can expose sensitive data.

- **Solution:** Use Azure Disk Encryption, Azure SQL Database Transparent Data Encryption, and Azure Storage Service Encryption to encrypt data at rest. Utilize Azure VPN or Azure ExpressRoute for secure data transit.

4. Compliance and Regulations:

- **Challenge:** Ensuring compliance with industry-specific regulations and standards can be challenging in a cloud environment.

- **Solution:** Leverage Azure's compliance certifications and features, such as Azure Policy and Azure Blueprints, to help meet regulatory requirements.

5. Data Loss Prevention:

- **Challenge:** Preventing accidental data loss is essential, as employees may unintentionally expose sensitive information.

- **Solution:** Implement Azure Information Protection to classify and protect sensitive data. Educate users about data handling best practices.

6. Insider Threats:

- **Challenge:** Insider threats, whether intentional or accidental, can compromise data security.

- **Solution:** Implement user and entity behavior analytics (UEBA) to detect unusual user activities. Set up alerts and triggers for suspicious activities.

7. Secure Development Practices:

- **Challenge:** Developing secure cloud-based applications and services is a priority.

- **Solution:** Follow Azure's secure development best practices and use tools like Azure DevOps to automate security testing in your CI/CD pipeline.

8. Shared Responsibility Model:

- **Challenge:** Understanding the shared responsibility model is crucial. Cloud providers secure the infrastructure, but users are responsible for securing their data and configurations.

- **Solution:** Clearly define the division of responsibilities and implement your part of the security controls.

9. Data Visibility:

- **Challenge:** Maintaining visibility into data and resource usage can be challenging.

- **Solution:** Utilize Azure Monitor and Azure Security Center for centralized monitoring, logging, and alerts.

10. Security Patching:

- **Challenge:** Keeping cloud resources up to date with security patches is essential.

- **Solution:** Implement automated patch management solutions for virtual machines and other resources.

By understanding these cloud data security challenges and adopting appropriate solutions, organizations can better secure their data in the cloud. Azure provides a range of security features and best practices to help mitigate these challenges and enhance data security in the cloud environment.

Azure Security Features

Microsoft Azure provides a wide range of security features to help protect your data and applications in the cloud. These features are designed to address various aspects of cloud security, including identity and access management, data protection, threat detection, and compliance. In this section, we'll explore some of the key Azure security features and how to leverage them to enhance the security of your cloud resources.

1. Azure Active Directory (Azure AD):

   - **Overview:** Azure AD is Microsoft's cloud-based identity and access management service. It provides features for managing user identities and controlling access to Azure resources.

   - **How to Use It:** You can use Azure AD to centralize identity management, implement single sign-on (SSO), and enforce multi-factor authentication (MFA) to enhance user authentication.

2. Role-Based Access Control (RBAC):

   - **Overview:** RBAC is an authorization system that allows you to control access to Azure resources by defining roles and assigning them to users or groups.

   - **How to Use It:** Implement RBAC to define granular access permissions for your resources. Assign roles like owner, contributor, or reader based on user responsibilities.

3. Azure Key Vault:

   - **Overview:** Azure Key Vault is a cloud-based service that allows you to securely manage keys, secrets, and certificates.

   - **How to Use It:** Store and manage sensitive information, such as API keys and connection strings, in Azure Key Vault to protect them from unauthorized access.

4. Azure Security Center:

   - **Overview:** Azure Security Center provides unified security management and advanced threat protection for Azure resources.

   - **How to Use It:** Monitor your cloud environment for security threats, apply security policies, and get recommendations for improving your security posture.

5. Azure Firewall:

   - **Overview:** Azure Firewall is a managed network security service that protects your Azure virtual network resources.

- How to Use It: Deploy Azure Firewall to control traffic flow and implement network rules to allow or deny specific traffic.

6. Azure DDoS Protection:

- Overview: Azure Distributed Denial of Service (DDoS) Protection safeguards your applications from DDoS attacks.

- How to Use It: Enable DDoS Protection for your Azure resources to mitigate the impact of DDoS attacks and maintain application availability.

7. Azure Policy:

- Overview: Azure Policy is a service that helps you enforce organizational standards and compliance for your resources.

- How to Use It: Define and assign policies to resources to ensure they adhere to your organization's requirements and compliance standards.

8. Azure Information Protection:

- Overview: Azure Information Protection helps classify, label, and protect sensitive information based on policies.

- How to Use It: Apply labels to documents and emails to enforce encryption and access restrictions for sensitive data.

9. Azure Sentinel:

- Overview: Azure Sentinel is a cloud-native security information and event management (SIEM) service that helps you detect, investigate, and respond to security threats.

- How to Use It: Use Azure Sentinel to collect security data, detect anomalies, and create custom alerts for security incidents.

10. Azure Virtual Network Security:

- **Overview:** Azure allows you to secure your virtual networks using features like Network Security Groups (NSGs) and Azure Firewall.

- **How to Use It:** Implement NSGs and Azure Firewall to filter network traffic and protect your virtual network resources.

These Azure security features provide a strong foundation for securing your cloud resources. By strategically implementing these features, you can enhance the overall security of your Azure-based applications and data. Additionally, regular monitoring and compliance checks are essential for maintaining a secure cloud environment.

Power BI Data Security Best Practices

Power BI offers a range of features and best practices to help you secure your data and reports in the cloud. Whether you're working with sensitive business information or confidential data, implementing these practices will help ensure that your data remains protected. Here are some best practices for securing your data in Power BI:

1. Authentication and Authorization:

- **Row-level Security:** Use Power BI's row-level security feature to restrict data access based on user roles or attributes. You can define security roles and filters to limit what data each user can see.

- **Azure AD Integration:** Leverage Azure Active Directory for user authentication. Ensure that only authorized users can access your Power BI content.

2. Encryption:

- **Data Encryption:** Enable data encryption at rest and in transit. Power BI supports encryption of data in datasets and during data transfer.

- **SSL Certificates:** Use SSL certificates to encrypt data communication between Power BI clients and the service.

3. Publish to Web:

- **Avoid Publish to Web:** Do not use the "Publish to Web" feature for sharing reports with sensitive data. This feature makes your reports public, and data may be accessible by anyone with the link.

4. Power BI Service Security Settings:

- **Configure Security Settings:** Adjust security settings in the Power BI service, such as controlling access to export data or print reports.

- **Data Classification:** Classify your data to indicate its sensitivity level. This helps users understand the data's importance and handle it accordingly.

5. Data Source Security:

- **Secure Data Sources:** Ensure that your data sources, such as databases or cloud storage, have proper security measures in place. Implement secure access controls and encryption where necessary.

6. Content Sharing:

- **Share Securely:** When sharing reports, be cautious about the sharing settings. Use secure sharing options like sharing with specific users or groups.

- **Embed in Apps:** For embedding reports in custom applications or websites, follow secure embedding practices and use secure tokens.

7. Compliance and Auditing:

- **Compliance Center:** Regularly review the Power BI Compliance Center for audit logs and compliance reports. Stay informed about activities and potential issues.

- **Data Governance:** Establish data governance policies to ensure that data remains compliant with your organization's regulations.

8. Keep Software Updated:

- **Stay Current:** Keep your Power BI Desktop and service up to date with the latest security patches and updates.

9. User Training:

- **User Education:** Train your users about data security best practices within Power BI. Ensure that they understand how to handle data securely.

10. Data Retention Policies:

- **Set Data Retention Policies:** Define data retention policies for your datasets and reports. Automatically remove or archive old data to minimize security risks.

These Power BI data security best practices help you maintain the confidentiality and integrity of your data. By implementing a combination of security features and user education, you can safeguard your data and reports while making the most of Power BI's capabilities.

8.2 Role-Based Access Control in Azure

Managing Access with Azure RBAC

Azure Role-Based Access Control (RBAC) is a crucial component of managing access to Azure resources, including those used in conjunction with Power BI. RBAC helps you control who has access to what resources and what actions they can perform. Let's delve into the details of managing access with Azure RBAC:

1. Azure RBAC Overview:

- Azure RBAC is an authorization system that defines the actions a user, group, or application can perform on Azure resources. Roles are predefined sets of permissions for various Azure services.

2. Predefined Roles:

- Azure provides several built-in roles such as Owner, Contributor, Reader, and many more. These roles encompass various levels of access control.

- *Owner*: Has full control over the resources, including managing access.

- *Contributor*: Can manage resources but not access control.

- *Reader*: Can view resources but not make any changes.

3. Custom Roles:

- You can create custom roles to tailor access control to your specific requirements. Custom roles allow you to define a precise set of permissions.

4. Assigning Roles:

- Access is granted by assigning roles to users, groups, or applications at different scopes, like subscription, resource group, or specific resources.

- You can assign multiple roles to a user or group within the same scope.

5. Azure Policy:

- Azure Policy is another tool that can work in conjunction with RBAC. Policies enforce compliance with your organizational standards.

6. Implementing Security Policies:

- Define security policies that specify which users or groups should have access to Power BI resources in Azure, and what actions they are allowed to perform.

- Implement the principle of least privilege to grant only the necessary permissions.

7. Fine-Grained Access Control in Power BI:

- Ensure that your Azure RBAC configurations align with the fine-grained access control settings in Power BI.

- Power BI's Row-Level Security and dataset-level roles allow you to further restrict data access within Power BI reports and dashboards.

8. Practical Example:

- Suppose you have a team of data analysts who need access to specific Power BI datasets and reports in the Azure cloud.

- You can create a custom RBAC role that grants read access to the Power BI resources within a specific resource group.

- Assign this custom role to the data analyst group.

9. Monitoring and Auditing:

- Continuously monitor and audit who has access to Power BI resources through Azure RBAC.

- Use Azure Activity Log and Azure Monitor to keep track of user actions and access changes.

By mastering Azure RBAC, you can manage access to Power BI and other Azure resources efficiently, ensuring that only authorized users can interact with your data and reports. It's a fundamental aspect of maintaining a secure and compliant environment.

Implementing Security Policies

Implementing security policies is a critical aspect of ensuring the safety of your data and resources in the Azure environment. These policies help define and enforce the security measures and practices that your organization needs to follow. Let's explore how to implement security policies effectively:

1. Azure Policy Overview:

- Azure Policy is a service that you can use to create, assign, and manage policies to enforce different rules and effects over your resources.

- Policies can ensure compliance with your company's standards, regulatory requirements, and security best practices.

2. Policy Definitions:

- Policy definitions are JSON files that specify the rules and effects that are enforced. They define what is allowed and what isn't.

3. Built-In and Custom Policies:

- Azure provides several built-in policies for common compliance requirements, such as requiring encryption of data.

- You can also create custom policies tailored to your organization's specific needs.

4. Initiatives:

- Initiatives are sets of policies that are grouped together to address a broader objective or compliance standard.

5. Assignment:

- Policies are assigned at a specific scope, such as a management group, subscription, or resource group.

- Policies are evaluated automatically as resources are created or updated.

6. Effects:

- Policies have effects, which can be either 'Deny' or 'Audit.'

- A 'Deny' effect restricts actions that are not compliant with the policy.

- An 'Audit' effect logs non-compliant actions but doesn't block them.

7. Practical Implementation:

- Consider a scenario where your organization wants to ensure that all virtual machines (VMs) are encrypted at rest.

- You can create a custom policy definition that checks if the 'encryption at rest' setting is enabled for VMs.

- Assign this policy at the appropriate scope (e.g., subscription) and set the effect to 'Deny.'

- When someone attempts to create an unencrypted VM, the policy will deny the action.

8. Continuous Compliance Monitoring:

   - Regularly review policy compliance results to ensure that resources remain compliant.

   - Monitor the audit logs and non-compliance events to identify issues that need attention.

9. Integration with Azure RBAC:

   - Policies and Azure Role-Based Access Control (RBAC) often work together. Policies can enforce security rules, while RBAC controls who has access to resources.

10. Third-Party Compliance Standards:

   - Azure Policy supports a wide range of compliance standards, including HIPAA, PCI, and more. You can use these built-in policies to adhere to specific regulations.

By implementing security policies in Azure, you can maintain a secure and compliant cloud environment. This ensures that your Azure resources, including those used in conjunction with Power BI, meet the necessary security standards and protect sensitive data effectively.

Fine-grained Access Control in Power BI

Fine-grained access control in Power BI allows you to precisely manage and restrict access to reports, datasets, and dashboards. This level of control is essential to maintain data security and comply with privacy regulations. Here's a comprehensive guide on how to implement fine-grained access control in Power BI:

1. Role-Based Permissions:

   - Power BI uses role-based permissions to control access. There are several predefined roles, including Viewer, Member, Contributor, and Admin.

2. Datasets and Reports:

- In Power BI, datasets are at the core of your reports and dashboards. Fine-grained access control begins with managing access to datasets.

- You can assign different roles to users or groups at the dataset level. For example, you can grant read-only access to a dataset for some users and full edit access to others.

3. Report-Level Permissions:

- Beyond datasets, you can also set permissions at the report level. This allows you to control who can view and modify specific reports.

- By defining roles and assigning users, you can customize access to reports within a dataset.

4. Row-Level Security (RLS):

- Row-Level Security is a powerful feature in Power BI that enables you to restrict data within a dataset.

- With RLS, you can define filters that control which data rows users can access. For instance, you can ensure that each user only sees their own data.

5. Integration with Azure Active Directory:

- Power BI's fine-grained access control can be integrated with Azure Active Directory (Azure AD). This simplifies user management and ensures consistent access policies.

6. Practical Implementation:

- Imagine a sales organization using Power BI for reporting. You can set up fine-grained access control as follows:

- Assign 'Sales Managers' to a dataset with full edit access.

- Assign 'Sales Representatives' to the same dataset with read-only access.

- Implement RLS to ensure that each sales representative can only see data relevant to their territory.

- Control report-level access, allowing managers to view additional reports.

7. Monitoring and Auditing:

  - Regularly audit permissions to ensure they align with your organization's requirements.

  - Use Power BI's audit logs to track user activity and detect any anomalies.

8. Best Practices:

  - Develop a clear access control policy, defining who gets access to what.

  - Regularly review and update permissions as roles within your organization change.

  - Document your access control settings for compliance purposes.

9. Training and Documentation:

  - Ensure that users are trained in the proper use of Power BI's access control features.

  - Create documentation to guide both administrators and users on managing permissions.

Fine-grained access control in Power BI empowers you to provide the right level of access to the right people while safeguarding sensitive data. This level of control is especially important when dealing with confidential information or when you need to comply with regulatory standards.

8.3 Compliance and Governance with Power BI and Azure

Achieving Regulatory Compliance

Ensuring regulatory compliance is critical for organizations that handle sensitive data. In the context of Power BI and Azure, compliance encompasses meeting the legal requirements and industry standards governing data privacy, security, and governance. Below are steps to achieve regulatory compliance:

1. Identify Applicable Regulations:

   - Begin by identifying the specific regulations or standards that pertain to your organization. These might include GDPR, HIPAA, SOX, or industry-specific regulations.

2. Data Classification:

   - Classify your data according to its sensitivity. This will help you determine the level of protection and access control required for different types of data.

3. Encryption:

   - Implement encryption mechanisms for data at rest and in transit. Azure offers encryption services like Azure Disk Encryption and Azure Storage Service Encryption.

4. Access Control:

   - Utilize role-based access control (RBAC) and fine-grained access control to restrict access to data, reports, and dashboards.

5. Data Governance in Azure:

- Implement Azure Policy and Azure Blueprints to ensure your resources in Azure comply with your organization's standards and policies.

6. Compliance Assessments:

- Regularly assess your Azure and Power BI environment for compliance with applicable regulations. Azure Policy can be used to automate compliance checks.

7. Audit and Logging:

- Enable auditing and logging in Azure to track who accesses your resources and what they do with them. Azure Monitor and Azure Security Center provide robust logging capabilities.

8. Privacy by Design:

- Embrace a "privacy by design" approach, which means considering data protection and privacy from the outset when designing and implementing your solutions.

9. Data Masking and Redaction:

- Implement data masking and redaction to protect sensitive data. Power BI offers features to anonymize or obfuscate data in your reports and dashboards.

10. Compliance Reporting:

- Use Power BI's capabilities for compliance reporting. You can create dashboards and reports that show the status of your compliance with various regulations and standards.

11. Training and Awareness:

- Train your team and employees about the importance of compliance and their role in maintaining it.

12. Third-Party Audits:

   - Consider third-party audits and certifications to validate your compliance efforts. Azure offers certifications for various standards.

13. Documentation:

   - Maintain detailed documentation of your compliance efforts, including policies, procedures, and audit reports.

14. Continuous Improvement:

   - Compliance is an ongoing process. Continuously monitor, assess, and improve your compliance measures as regulations evolve and your organization's needs change.

15. Legal Counsel:

   - Consult legal counsel experienced in data privacy and compliance to ensure you are meeting all legal requirements.

Achieving regulatory compliance is not a one-time effort but an ongoing commitment to safeguarding data and meeting the expectations of governing bodies. By following these steps, you can establish a strong compliance framework within your Power BI and Azure environments.

Implementing Data Governance in Azure

Implementing robust data governance practices in Azure is essential for maintaining data quality, security, and compliance. It helps organizations establish processes and guidelines for data handling, usage, and access control. Here's a comprehensive guide on how to implement data governance in Azure:

1. Define Data Governance Framework:

- Start by defining a data governance framework that outlines your organization's data policies, procedures, and standards. This framework should include roles and responsibilities.

2. Data Classification:

- Classify your data into different categories based on sensitivity and usage. Identify critical data that requires special protection.

3. Data Catalog:

- Implement a data catalog or metadata repository where you document data assets, including data sources, data types, and ownership.

4. Data Quality Management:

- Establish processes for data quality management, including data profiling, cleansing, and validation. Azure Data Factory and Azure Databricks can help with data quality tasks.

5. Access Control:

- Utilize Azure RBAC (Role-Based Access Control) to manage access to Azure resources. Define roles and assign permissions based on job functions.

6. Data Encryption:

- Implement encryption for sensitive data at rest and in transit using Azure services like Azure Disk Encryption, Azure Storage Service Encryption, and Azure Key Vault.

7. Data Masking and Redaction:

- Apply data masking and redaction techniques to hide sensitive information in reports and dashboards. Power BI offers features for this purpose.

8. Data Retention and Deletion:

   - Define policies for data retention and deletion. Use Azure Blob Storage lifecycle management to automatically delete data when it's no longer needed.

9. Audit and Monitoring:

   - Enable auditing and monitoring in Azure using Azure Monitor, Azure Security Center, and Azure Sentinel. Track data access and changes for compliance and security.

10. Data Lineage and Data Flow:

   - Document data lineage and data flow within your Azure environment to understand how data moves through your system.

11. Data Catalog and Data Discovery:

   - Use Azure Data Catalog or other data catalog solutions to provide a searchable inventory of your data assets.

12. Data Ownership and Stewardship:

   - Assign data owners and stewards who are responsible for data quality, access control, and compliance.

13. Data Compliance Reporting:

   - Develop compliance reports and dashboards using Power BI to provide insights into your data governance efforts.

14. Training and Awareness:

   - Train your staff and end-users on data governance principles, policies, and practices. Encourage data stewardship.

15. Compliance with Regulations:

- Ensure that your data governance practices align with relevant regulations such as GDPR, HIPAA, and industry-specific standards.

16. Regular Audits:

- Conduct regular audits to assess the effectiveness of your data governance processes. Make improvements as needed.

17. Data Governance Tools:

- Consider using Azure Purview (formerly Azure Data Catalog) and other data governance tools to automate and streamline data governance tasks.

By implementing data governance in Azure, you can maintain data integrity, protect sensitive information, ensure regulatory compliance, and make data-driven decisions with confidence. This comprehensive approach will help you manage your data assets effectively within the Azure ecosystem.

Data Auditing and Compliance Reporting in Power BI

Auditing and compliance reporting in Power BI are crucial components of a robust data governance strategy. These processes help organizations track data usage, ensure compliance with regulatory requirements, and maintain data integrity. Here's a detailed guide on how to perform data auditing and compliance reporting in Power BI:

1. Data Auditing in Power BI:

- Data auditing involves tracking and recording activities related to your Power BI datasets, reports, and dashboards. To enable auditing in Power BI, follow these steps:

a. Enable Auditing in Power BI Service:

- Log in to the Power BI service and go to the admin portal.

- In the "Audit settings" section, enable auditing. You can configure which activities to audit, such as dataset views, report interactions, and data export.

b. Configure Audit Logs:

- Define the location where audit logs will be stored, such as an Azure Storage Account or an Office 365 Security & Compliance Center.

c. Retrieve Audit Logs:

- Use Power BI REST APIs to retrieve audit logs programmatically. You can also use PowerShell scripts to automate this process.

2. Compliance Reporting:

- Compliance reporting ensures that your Power BI implementation complies with industry standards and regulatory requirements. Here's how to create compliance reports:

a. Define Compliance Requirements:

- Identify the compliance standards or regulations relevant to your organization, such as GDPR, HIPAA, or industry-specific standards.

b. Data Classification:

- Classify your data into different categories based on sensitivity and compliance requirements.

c. Report Templates:

- Create compliance report templates that include the necessary elements for each regulation or standard. These elements may include data protection policies, data access logs, and data encryption measures.

d. Data Access Controls:

- Implement role-based access control (RBAC) in Power BI to restrict data access to authorized users.

e. Data Encryption:

- Encrypt sensitive data within your Power BI reports and datasets. Power BI offers encryption options to protect data at rest and in transit.

f. Audit Data Access:

- Use the audit logs collected in the previous step to track data access and usage. Ensure that only authorized users access sensitive data.

g. Generate Compliance Reports:

- Use Power BI's report authoring capabilities to create compliance reports. You can include visualizations, tables, and narratives that explain how your data governance measures align with compliance requirements.

h. Automation:

- Consider automating compliance report generation using Power BI APIs or scheduled data refresh.

3. Data Auditing and Compliance Tools:

- There are several tools and services available to assist with data auditing and compliance reporting in Power BI:

a. Power BI REST APIs: These APIs allow you to retrieve audit logs and perform other administrative tasks programmatically.

b. PowerShell Scripts: PowerShell can be used to automate data auditing and compliance reporting tasks, including log retrieval and report generation.

4. Regular Audits:

- Conduct regular audits to ensure ongoing compliance. Review your compliance reports, and make any necessary adjustments to your data governance practices to address non-compliance issues.

By following these steps, you can effectively perform data auditing and compliance reporting in Power BI, helping your organization maintain regulatory compliance and data security. These practices contribute to a comprehensive data governance strategy in your Power BI and Azure environment.

CHAPTER VIII
Power BI in Business Scenarios

9.1 Case Study 1: Building a Cloud-based Business Analytics Platform

Business Goals and Requirements

In this section, we will delve into the business goals and requirements of our case study, "Building a Cloud-based Business Analytics Platform." It's essential to understand the objectives and prerequisites before designing and implementing any analytics solution. The business goals and requirements serve as the foundation for the entire project.

1. Business Goals:

- Enhanced Decision-Making: The primary goal of this project is to enable data-driven decision-making. The organization aims to make more informed, strategic decisions by leveraging data and analytics.

- Cost Reduction: There is a desire to optimize operational costs by identifying inefficiencies and areas where cost reduction is possible.

- Revenue Growth: Increasing revenue and identifying new revenue streams is another business goal. This involves identifying market opportunities and customer segments.

- Competitive Advantage: The organization seeks a competitive edge by being more agile and responsive in the market.

2. Business Requirements:

- Data Integration: The company requires the ability to integrate data from various sources, including on-premises databases, cloud sources, and external data providers.

- Data Quality: Ensuring data quality is a top requirement. Data should be accurate, consistent, and up-to-date.

- Scalability: As the organization grows, the analytics platform must be scalable to handle increasing data volumes and user demands.

- Real-time Analytics: The business requires real-time or near-real-time analytics capabilities for monitoring and responding to changing market conditions promptly.

- Self-service Analytics: Empowering business users with self-service analytics tools to explore data and generate insights without heavy reliance on IT.

- Data Security and Compliance: Compliance with industry regulations (e.g., GDPR, HIPAA) and data security are paramount.

- User Training and Adoption: Ensuring that users are trained and comfortable using the analytics platform is a requirement for this project's success.

3. Key Performance Indicators (KPIs):

- The organization has defined KPIs to measure the success of the project, including metrics related to cost reduction, revenue growth, data accuracy, and user adoption.

4. Stakeholder Involvement:

- Various stakeholders from different departments, including IT, business operations, and data analytics, are involved in this project. Collaborative efforts are essential to meet the business goals and requirements.

By clearly defining these business goals and requirements, the organization sets the stage for a successful analytics platform implementation. In the next sections, we will explore the architecture and implementation of this cloud-based business analytics platform and the outcomes and benefits it brings to the organization.

Architecture and Implementation

In this section, we will explore the architecture and implementation of the cloud-based business analytics platform as outlined in Case Study 1: "Building a Cloud-based Business Analytics Platform."

1. Cloud Platform Selection:

The first step in the architecture and implementation process is selecting a cloud platform that aligns with the business goals and requirements. Based on the case study, let's assume Azure was chosen as the cloud provider due to its robust analytics and data processing capabilities.

2. Data Ingestion and Integration:

- Data Sources: The platform begins with identifying and connecting various data sources, which can include on-premises databases, external APIs, and cloud-based data stores.

- Azure Data Factory: Azure Data Factory is utilized for data integration. It enables data pipelines to move data from various sources to a central data repository.

3. Data Storage and Warehousing:

- Azure Data Lake Storage: The platform uses Azure Data Lake Storage as a data repository for storing raw and processed data. Data Lake Storage offers scalability, data security, and analytics capabilities.

- Azure Synapse Analytics: For data warehousing and advanced analytics, Azure Synapse Analytics (formerly SQL Data Warehouse) is implemented. It provides the ability to process large volumes of data and perform complex queries.

4. Data Transformation and ETL:

- Azure Databricks: Azure Databricks, an Apache Spark-based analytics platform, is used for data transformation and ETL (Extract, Transform, Load) processes. Databricks provides an environment for data engineering and machine learning tasks.

5. Data Modeling:

- Azure SQL Data Warehouse: Azure SQL Data Warehouse stores curated and transformed data. Business analysts and data scientists can use it to build data models.

6. Data Visualization and Reporting:

- Power BI: Power BI, a business intelligence tool by Microsoft, is used for data visualization and reporting. It allows creating interactive and shareable dashboards and reports.

7. Real-time Analytics:

- Azure Stream Analytics: For real-time analytics, Azure Stream Analytics is employed to process and analyze streaming data from IoT devices or other sources.

8. Security and Compliance:

- Azure Security Center: Azure Security Center is utilized to monitor and protect the cloud environment, ensuring data security and compliance with industry standards.

9. User Training and Adoption:

- To ensure successful user adoption, training sessions and documentation are provided to users, enabling them to make the most of the platform.

10. Automation and Scaling:

- The architecture is designed for automation and scaling. Azure's autoscaling features are configured to handle increased workloads and data volumes.

11. Ongoing Monitoring:

- Continuous monitoring is in place to track the platform's performance, security, and adherence to compliance requirements.

12. Outcome and Benefits:

The outcomes and benefits of this architecture and implementation will be discussed in the following section of the case study. This will include insights into how the platform helped achieve the business goals and requirements outlined earlier.

By effectively designing and implementing the architecture as described, the organization is well-positioned to leverage data and analytics to make data-driven decisions, reduce costs, grow revenue, gain a competitive advantage, and ensure data security and compliance. The specific benefits and results of this implementation will be explored in the next part of the case study.

Outcomes and Benefits

In this section, we will delve into the outcomes and benefits achieved through the implementation of the cloud-based business analytics platform as described in Case Study 1.

1. Enhanced Data-Driven Decision Making:

The implementation of the analytics platform has empowered the organization to make data-driven decisions with increased accuracy and confidence. Business analysts and decision-makers now have access to real-time and historical data, which enables them to identify trends, patterns, and critical insights for informed decision-making.

2. Improved Business Agility:

The platform's scalability and real-time analytics capabilities have improved the organization's agility. It can quickly adapt to changing market conditions, customer preferences, and business requirements. The ability to process and analyze data at scale allows for rapid responses to emerging opportunities and challenges.

3. Cost Reduction:

The architecture and implementation have led to cost reductions in several ways:

- Data Processing Efficiency: By optimizing data processing and leveraging cloud resources efficiently, the organization has reduced operational costs.

- Legacy System Decommissioning: The migration to the cloud and consolidation of data sources has allowed the organization to decommission costly legacy systems, saving on maintenance and infrastructure expenses.

4. Revenue Growth:

Through data-driven insights, the organization has identified new revenue opportunities, cross-selling possibilities, and enhanced customer experiences. The ability to analyze customer behavior and preferences in real-time has resulted in targeted marketing campaigns and increased sales.

5. Competitive Advantage:

The business analytics platform has given the organization a competitive advantage. It can respond to market changes faster than competitors, tailor its offerings to customer needs, and maintain a high level of service quality.

6. Enhanced Security and Compliance:

The implementation of Azure Security Center and adherence to best practices have enhanced data security and ensured compliance with industry regulations and standards. This has resulted in a reduced risk of data breaches and regulatory penalties.

7. User Adoption and Satisfaction:

The availability of Power BI for data visualization and reporting has made data analysis more accessible to business users. The organization has observed improved user adoption and satisfaction as users can create their dashboards and reports without extensive technical knowledge.

8. Scalability and Performance:

The platform's architecture supports scaling based on workloads, ensuring that it can handle growing data volumes and increasing processing demands without compromising performance.

9. Data Auditing and Compliance Reporting:

Data auditing and compliance reporting in Power BI have facilitated transparency and accountability. The organization can demonstrate compliance with regulatory requirements, providing assurance to stakeholders and auditors.

10. Business Continuity:

With data redundancies and disaster recovery measures in place, the organization has established robust business continuity strategies, reducing the risk of data loss and downtime.

11. Return on Investment (ROI):

The outcomes and benefits detailed above have contributed to a positive return on investment (ROI). The initial investment in building the cloud-based business analytics platform has yielded financial rewards and continues to provide long-term value.

Overall, the organization has realized substantial gains in terms of data utilization, operational efficiency, cost management, and competitive positioning. The cloud-based business analytics platform has become a critical asset in achieving business goals and maintaining a competitive edge in the market.

9.2 Case Study 2: IoT Data Analytics with Power BI and Azure

IoT Data Sources and Challenges

In Case Study 2, we explore the world of IoT (Internet of Things) data analytics and how Power BI and Azure services can be harnessed to extract valuable insights. The initial phase of the case study focuses on understanding the various IoT data sources and the challenges that organizations face in effectively harnessing this data for decision-making.

IoT Data Sources:

IoT data can originate from a wide range of sources, each of which contributes unique datasets to the analytics ecosystem. Some common IoT data sources include:

1. Sensors and Devices: IoT devices equipped with sensors generate data related to temperature, humidity, pressure, motion, location, and various environmental conditions.

2. Industrial Equipment: In manufacturing and industrial settings, machinery and equipment collect data on performance, maintenance needs, and operational efficiency.

3. Connected Vehicles: IoT data from vehicles includes information on location, speed, engine performance, fuel consumption, and more.

4. Smart Home Devices: Devices like thermostats, security cameras, and voice assistants generate data on home automation and security.

5. Wearable Devices: Wearables track health metrics such as heart rate, sleep patterns, and exercise data.

6. Environmental Sensors: These sensors monitor air quality, pollution levels, and weather conditions.

Challenges in IoT Data Analytics:

While IoT data offers significant opportunities, it also presents several challenges:

1. Data Volume: IoT devices generate massive amounts of data. Handling and processing this volume efficiently is a significant challenge.

2. Data Variety: IoT data is diverse, comprising structured and unstructured data, time-series data, and geospatial data. Integrating and analyzing such varied data types can be complex.

3. Real-time Processing: Many IoT applications require real-time or near-real-time data processing and analysis to respond quickly to events.

4. Data Quality: Ensuring data quality and accuracy is essential for reliable insights. Noisy or inaccurate data can lead to incorrect conclusions.

5. Security and Privacy: IoT data often contains sensitive information, making security and privacy crucial concerns. Unauthorized access or data breaches could have severe consequences.

6. Scalability: Scalability is vital to accommodate the growing number of IoT devices and the increasing data load.

7. Complexity of Analytics: Creating meaningful insights from IoT data involves advanced analytics, machine learning, and predictive modeling.

8. Data Integration: IoT data often needs to be integrated with existing data sources for comprehensive analysis. Achieving this seamlessly can be challenging.

In the following sections of this case study, we will explore how Azure services and Power BI address these challenges, enabling organizations to extract valuable insights from their IoT data sources. This includes real-time data processing, advanced analytics, and visualization techniques that empower decision-makers to respond to IoT data in a timely and informed manner.

IoT Data Processing with Azure Services

In this section of Case Study 2, we will delve into the critical process of processing IoT (Internet of Things) data using Azure services. Azure offers a comprehensive suite of services designed to collect, ingest, process, and analyze IoT data efficiently.

1. Data Ingestion:

The first step in IoT data processing is ingesting data from various sources into the Azure environment. Azure provides services such as Azure IoT Hub and Azure Event Hubs to collect data from IoT devices in real-time. These services offer scalability and can handle large volumes of data.

2. Data Storage:

Once data is ingested, it needs to be stored in a scalable and reliable manner. Azure offers several options for this:

- Azure Blob Storage: Azure Blob Storage is a highly scalable object storage service that can store unstructured data, including IoT data. It provides redundancy and data protection.

- Azure Data Lake Storage: Azure Data Lake Storage Gen2 is a large-scale data lake solution for big data analytics. It's designed for high-speed data processing and supports various data types.

- Azure SQL Database: For structured data, Azure SQL Database is an option. It provides a managed database service with built-in intelligence.

3. Data Processing:

Azure offers several services for processing IoT data efficiently:

- Azure Stream Analytics: This real-time data stream processing service enables the transformation and analysis of data as it arrives. It supports complex event processing, temporal windowing, and integration with Power BI.

- Azure Functions: Serverless computing with Azure Functions allows you to run code in response to events or triggers. This can be used for data processing tasks.

- Azure Databricks: For advanced data analytics, including machine learning and AI, Azure Databricks is a collaborative Apache Spark-based analytics platform.

4. Data Analytics:

Azure services support the analysis of IoT data through various tools and frameworks:

- Azure Machine Learning: This platform allows data scientists and engineers to build, train, and deploy machine learning models on IoT data for predictive analytics.

- Power BI: Power BI is a business analytics tool that provides interactive data visualization and business intelligence capabilities. It can connect to Azure services to create real-time dashboards and reports.

5. Real-time IoT Analytics with Power BI:

The final step is real-time IoT analytics. Power BI, when connected to Azure services like Azure Stream Analytics, can display real-time data insights through interactive dashboards and reports. This empowers decision-makers to monitor and respond to IoT data in real-time, improving situational awareness and enabling timely actions.

In the next section, we will explore how to achieve real-time IoT analytics with Power BI, illustrating this process with practical examples and code explanations. This will allow organizations to harness the power of IoT data for informed decision-making.

Real-time IoT Analytics with Power BI

In this section, we will explore the process of achieving real-time IoT analytics with Power BI integrated with Azure services. Real-time IoT analytics is a critical aspect of harnessing the power of IoT data to make informed decisions and take timely actions.

1. Power BI Integration with Azure Services:

Before diving into the practical steps, it's essential to highlight the integration points between Power BI and Azure services for real-time IoT analytics. The primary Azure service that plays a crucial role in this scenario is Azure Stream Analytics. Azure Stream Analytics is a real-time data stream processing service that can process and analyze incoming IoT data in real-time.

2. Data Ingestion and Processing:

The real-time IoT analytics process begins with the ingestion of data from IoT devices into Azure Stream Analytics. Azure Stream Analytics can connect to various IoT data sources, including Azure IoT Hub, Event Hubs, and custom data sources.

- Input Configuration: Start by configuring the input for Azure Stream Analytics, specifying the source of IoT data.

- Query Definition: Create a Stream Analytics query that defines how the incoming data should be processed. This includes filtering, transforming, and aggregating data as needed.

- Output Configuration: Configure the output of Azure Stream Analytics, which will be connected to Power BI for real-time visualization.

3. Power BI Dashboard Creation:

Now, let's create a Power BI dashboard to visualize real-time IoT data. Here are the steps:

- Connect to Azure Stream Analytics: In Power BI, use the Azure Stream Analytics connector to establish a connection with the output of your Azure Stream Analytics job.

- Data Transformation: Define data transformation and modeling within Power Query Editor in Power BI to ensure the data is structured for visualization.

- Real-time Dashboards: Create real-time dashboards in Power BI using features like streaming datasets and live tiles. These dashboards will update in real-time as new IoT data arrives.

- Visualizations: Design visualizations and charts to represent IoT data, such as line charts, gauges, maps, and more.

- Customization: Customize your dashboard to display critical IoT insights and KPIs that align with your specific use case.

4. Real-time Monitoring and Insights:

With the Power BI dashboard connected to Azure Stream Analytics, your organization can monitor IoT data in real-time, enabling you to gain immediate insights. These insights can drive actions, trigger alerts, and provide a clear view of IoT operations.

5. Example Code (Azure Stream Analytics Query):

Here's an example of a Stream Analytics query for processing IoT temperature data:

```sql
SELECT
    DeviceId,
    System.Timestamp AS EventTime,
    Temperature
INTO
    PowerBIOutput
FROM
    IoTHubInput
WHERE
    Temperature > 25
```

This query selects temperature data from IoT devices, timestamps the events, and filters out data where the temperature is above 25 degrees. The processed data is sent to the Power BI output.

6. Conclusion:

Real-time IoT analytics with Power BI and Azure Stream Analytics empowers organizations to monitor, analyze, and act upon IoT data as it arrives. This capability is invaluable for use cases such as predictive maintenance, asset tracking, and quality control. In the next section, we will explore additional case studies and real-world examples to illustrate the practical application of this technology.

Stay tuned for Case Study 2's practical application of real-time IoT analytics in a real-world scenario.

9.3 Case Study 3: Healthcare Analytics in the Cloud

Healthcare Data Challenges

In the healthcare industry, data plays a crucial role in improving patient care, optimizing operations, and advancing medical research. However, healthcare data presents unique challenges, including privacy concerns, data volume, and interoperability. In this section, we will explore the challenges associated with healthcare data and how Azure and Power BI can address them.

1. Data Privacy and Compliance:

Challenge: Healthcare data, which includes patient records, diagnoses, and treatments, is highly sensitive and subject to strict privacy regulations, such as HIPAA (Health Insurance Portability and Accountability Act) in the United States. Healthcare organizations must ensure the confidentiality, integrity, and availability of patient data while complying with regulatory requirements.

Solution: Azure offers a range of services designed to help healthcare organizations manage and secure sensitive data. Azure Data Lake Storage and Azure SQL Database can be configured with advanced security features and compliance certifications to protect healthcare data. Additionally, Azure Key Vault provides secure key management and encryption.

2. Data Interoperability:

Challenge: Healthcare data often resides in different formats and systems, making data interoperability a significant challenge. Electronic health records (EHRs) may use different standards and structures, making it difficult to integrate data from various sources.

Solution: Azure Integration Services, such as Azure Logic Apps and Azure API Management, can facilitate the integration of disparate healthcare systems. They enable data to flow seamlessly between EHRs, laboratory systems, and other healthcare data sources. Power BI can then connect to these integrated data sources to provide insights and reports.

3. Data Volume and Scalability:

Challenge: Healthcare organizations generate large volumes of data, including medical images, sensor data, and patient records. Scaling to accommodate the growing data volume and ensuring that data is available when needed is a critical challenge.

Solution: Azure's cloud scalability is well-suited for healthcare data. Azure Cosmos DB can handle high-velocity data, while Azure Data Factory can automate data ingestion and processing. Azure Functions can be used for serverless computing, and Power BI can provide real-time insights from this large and growing dataset.

4. Data Quality and Accuracy:

Challenge: Healthcare data needs to be of the highest quality to ensure patient safety and accurate decision-making. Data inconsistencies or inaccuracies can have severe consequences.

Solution: Implement data quality checks and validation processes using Azure Data Factory and Azure Databricks. Power BI can create data quality reports and dashboards to monitor data accuracy, helping healthcare professionals make informed decisions.

5. Cost Management:

Challenge: Managing the cost of data storage, processing, and analytics in healthcare can be a concern, especially for organizations with tight budgets.

Solution: Azure's cost management tools, such as Azure Cost Management and Billing, can help healthcare organizations monitor and optimize their cloud expenses. By understanding resource usage, organizations can make informed decisions about scaling up or down to meet their budgetary requirements.

Addressing these challenges is crucial for healthcare organizations looking to leverage data for improved patient care, research, and operational efficiency. In the next sections, we will explore how Azure and Power BI can be implemented to securely store and process healthcare data, as well as provide insights and reporting for healthcare analytics. Stay tuned for insights into securing healthcare data and the secure data storage and processing capabilities of Azure.

Secure Data Storage and Processing in Azure

In the healthcare industry, ensuring the secure storage and processing of sensitive patient data is paramount. Azure provides a comprehensive set of services and features that can be leveraged to meet the stringent security and compliance requirements of healthcare data.

1. Data Storage in Azure:

- Azure Data Lake Storage: This is an ideal choice for secure and scalable data storage. Data Lake Storage provides fine-grained access control and encryption to protect sensitive healthcare data at rest.

- Azure SQL Database: For structured healthcare data, Azure SQL Database offers features like Transparent Data Encryption (TDE) and Always Encrypted, ensuring data remains confidential and is not exposed to unauthorized access.

- Azure Blob Storage: Azure Blob Storage provides an option for cost-effective storage of unstructured data, including medical images and documents. Data can be encrypted at rest using Azure's built-in encryption.

2. Data Encryption:

- Encryption in Transit: To protect data during transmission, use Azure Virtual Networks and Azure VPN Gateway to establish private connections. All data flowing through these networks is encrypted by default.

- Azure Disk Encryption: For virtual machines and storage, Azure Disk Encryption can be enabled to ensure that data remains encrypted even if hardware is compromised.

3. Identity and Access Management:

- Azure Active Directory: Securely manage user identities and access to Azure resources with Azure Active Directory (Azure AD). Implement Multi-Factor Authentication (MFA) to enhance security.

- Role-Based Access Control (RBAC): Use RBAC to assign specific permissions to users and groups, ensuring that only authorized personnel can access healthcare data.

4. Compliance and Auditing:

- Azure Policy and Blueprints: Define and enforce policies for compliance requirements. Create custom policies to ensure data is stored and accessed in accordance with regulatory standards.

- Azure Monitor and Azure Security Center: These services provide continuous monitoring and security assessments to detect and respond to threats in real time. They also help maintain compliance with security standards.

5. Data Processing:

- Azure Databricks: Leverage Azure Databricks for data processing and analytics. It offers built-in security features and is HIPAA-compliant, making it suitable for healthcare data processing.

- Azure Functions: Implement serverless computing with Azure Functions to process data without the need to manage infrastructure. This approach can ensure efficient and secure data processing.

6. Data Backups and Disaster Recovery:

- Azure Backup: Regularly back up healthcare data using Azure Backup, which provides a secure and reliable mechanism for data protection.

- Azure Site Recovery: Implement disaster recovery plans to ensure data availability in case of unexpected incidents.

7. Data Retention and De-Identification:

- Azure Purview (formerly Azure Data Catalog): Use Azure Purview to discover and classify sensitive healthcare data. Implement data retention policies and de-identification techniques to comply with regulations.

8. Monitoring and Alerts:

- Azure Security Center: Set up security alerts to receive notifications of potential security threats. Azure Security Center continuously monitors resources for potential vulnerabilities.

Securing healthcare data in Azure involves a combination of the services mentioned above and the development of robust security policies and practices. It's essential to work closely with legal and compliance teams to ensure that your healthcare organization's data storage and processing adhere to relevant regulations, such as HIPAA.

The next section will delve into leveraging Azure and Power BI for healthcare insights and reporting. Stay tuned for a detailed exploration of how these tools can empower healthcare professionals with data-driven decision-making capabilities.

Healthcare Insights and Reporting with Power BI

Power BI is a powerful tool for transforming healthcare data into actionable insights and reports. By connecting to various healthcare data sources, you can create dynamic and interactive reports that help healthcare professionals make informed decisions, track patient outcomes, and monitor hospital performance. In this section, we'll explore how to leverage Power BI for healthcare insights and reporting.

1. Data Source Integration:

- Connect to Healthcare Data: Power BI allows you to connect to a wide range of healthcare data sources, such as electronic health records (EHR) systems, healthcare databases, and IoT devices. Utilize connectors to establish secure connections and retrieve data.

2. Data Transformation and Cleaning:

- Data Cleaning: Perform data cleansing and transformation tasks to ensure that healthcare data is accurate and reliable. Address issues like missing values, duplicates, and outliers.

- Data Modeling: Create a robust data model that reflects healthcare domain knowledge. This includes defining relationships between tables, creating hierarchies, and implementing time intelligence for date-based analysis.

3. Healthcare Analytics:

- Patient Outcomes Analysis: Utilize Power BI to track patient outcomes, including recovery rates, readmission rates, and mortality rates. Visualize this data through interactive reports to identify trends and make data-driven clinical decisions.

- Clinical Performance Monitoring: Monitor the performance of healthcare facilities and staff. Track key performance indicators (KPIs) such as average waiting times, patient satisfaction scores, and resource utilization.

- Real-time Monitoring: For IoT and remote patient monitoring, implement real-time dashboards that display vital signs and other health-related data. Set up alerts for critical thresholds to ensure timely responses.

4. Healthcare Reporting:

- Patient Dashboards: Develop patient-facing dashboards that allow patients to access their own health records and gain insights into their well-being. Patient dashboards can include medication schedules, appointment reminders, and health goals.

- Physician Reports: Equip healthcare providers with custom reports that display patient histories, diagnoses, and treatment plans. These reports can enhance clinical decision-making.

- Compliance Reports: Generate regulatory compliance reports required by healthcare authorities, such as HIPAA compliance reports. Ensure that sensitive patient data is appropriately protected.

5. Visualizations:

- Custom Visualizations: Design custom visualizations tailored to healthcare needs. Examples include heat maps of disease outbreaks, geographic analyses, and patient journey diagrams.

- Predictive Analytics: Implement predictive models within Power BI to forecast patient volumes, resource requirements, or disease prevalence.

6. Security and Compliance:

- Row-Level Security: Use Power BI's row-level security features to ensure that only authorized users can access specific patient records.

- Data Encryption: Encrypt healthcare data within Power BI to protect against unauthorized access.

7. Integration with Azure Services:

- Integration with Azure Machine Learning: Embed machine learning models from Azure Machine Learning into Power BI reports for predictive analytics.

8. User Training and Adoption:

- Training for Healthcare Staff: Train healthcare professionals on how to use Power BI effectively. Ensure that users understand the reports and can navigate them easily.

9. Data Governance:

- Data Auditing: Implement data auditing to track changes to healthcare data and ensure data integrity.

10. Continuous Improvement:

- Feedback Mechanism: Establish a feedback mechanism to collect input from healthcare professionals and patients. Use this feedback to improve the quality and relevance of healthcare reports.

- Performance Monitoring: Monitor the performance and response times of Power BI reports to ensure that they meet the needs of healthcare providers.

By harnessing Power BI's capabilities, healthcare organizations can derive valuable insights, improve patient care, and enhance operational efficiency. This case study demonstrates the potential of using Power BI to empower healthcare professionals with the tools they need to deliver high-quality care while adhering to strict regulatory standards.

CHAPTER IX
Data Visualization and Reporting

10.1 Creating Interactive Dashboards and Reports

Designing Engaging Dashboards

Creating engaging dashboards is crucial for ensuring that your audience can quickly grasp the insights and information presented in your reports. Power BI provides a range of features and design best practices to help you design dashboards that are not only visually appealing but also effective in conveying information. In this section, we will explore the key considerations and steps for designing engaging dashboards in Power BI.

1. Understand Your Audience:

Before you start designing your dashboard, it's essential to understand who your audience is and what specific insights or information they need. Knowing your audience's needs and preferences will guide your design decisions.

2. Define Clear Objectives:

Set clear objectives for your dashboard. What story or message do you want to convey through the data? Having well-defined objectives will help you focus on what's essential and avoid clutter.

3. Data Selection and Preparation:

- Data Sources: Ensure you have a clear understanding of your data sources. Use Power Query to prepare and transform your data before importing it into Power BI.

- Data Model: Create a robust data model with well-defined relationships between tables. Optimize your data model for performance.

4. Layout and Composition:

- Grid System: Use a grid system to organize your dashboard elements. This ensures alignment and consistency in the layout.

- Visual Hierarchy: Establish a clear visual hierarchy for your dashboard. Important information should stand out, and less critical details should be visually de-emphasized.

- Whitespace: Leverage whitespace effectively to create a clean and uncluttered look. Adequate spacing between elements makes the dashboard more readable.

5. Color and Style:

- Color Palette: Select a suitable color palette that aligns with your organization's branding or the message you want to convey. Use colors consistently to represent similar data or categories.

- Fonts and Typography: Choose fonts that are easy to read and maintain consistency in font usage throughout the dashboard.

6. Visualizations:

- Select the Right Visuals: Choose the most appropriate visualizations for your data. Bar charts, line charts, pie charts, and maps are just a few of the options available in Power BI.

- Interactive Elements: Utilize interactive elements such as slicers, filters, and drill-through functionality to allow users to explore the data themselves.

7. Customization:

- Themes: Create or select a theme for your dashboard that matches your organization's branding. Power BI allows you to customize themes to maintain consistency.

- Custom Visuals: Explore custom visuals created by the Power BI community or develop your own if the standard visuals do not meet your requirements.

8. Storytelling:

- Narrative Flow: Design your dashboard to tell a story. Lead users through a sequence of visuals to help them understand the data and insights better.

- Annotations and Text Boxes: Use text boxes, annotations, and titles to add context and explanations to your visuals.

9. Responsiveness:

- Device-Friendly Design: Ensure your dashboard is responsive and looks good on different devices, including desktops, tablets, and mobile phones.

10. Testing and Iteration:

- Usability Testing: Gather feedback from potential users and stakeholders to identify areas for improvement.

- Iterate: Be prepared to iterate and refine your dashboard based on user feedback and changing data requirements.

Creating engaging dashboards in Power BI is a mix of art and science. It requires a deep understanding of your data, your audience, and the principles of data visualization and design. By following these best practices, you can create dashboards that effectively communicate insights and engage your audience.

Interactivity Features in Power BI

Power BI provides a variety of interactivity features that allow users to explore and interact with data in reports and dashboards. These features enhance the user experience and help convey insights more effectively. In this section, we will explore some of the key interactivity features available in Power BI.

1. Filters and Slicers:

- Usage: Filters and slicers allow users to narrow down data by selecting specific values or ranges. For example, users can filter data by date, category, region, or any other relevant dimension.

- How to Use: To add filters and slicers, you can use the "Filters" and "Slicers" visualizations available in Power BI. You can connect these visuals to other report elements to filter data based on user selections.

- Customization: You can customize the appearance and behavior of filters and slicers to match the dashboard's design and user preferences.

2. Drill-Through:

- Usage: Drill-through allows users to access more detailed information about a particular data point. For instance, users can drill through from a summary visual to a detailed report or page with relevant data.

- How to Use: You can set up drill-through actions in Power BI by defining fields and pages that users can navigate to when they drill through.

- Contextual Information: Drill-through can provide contextual information relevant to the selected data point, enhancing the user's understanding of the data.

3. Bookmarks and Buttons:

- Usage: Bookmarks and buttons enable the creation of interactive narratives or guided exploration in reports. Users can click buttons or bookmarks to jump to different parts of the report.

- How to Use: You can add bookmarks and buttons to your report by creating bookmarks and defining actions when users click on buttons. This is useful for storytelling and highlighting key insights.

- Annotations: Annotations can be added to bookmarks to provide explanations or context for specific sections of the report.

4. Cross-Filtering and Highlighting:

- Usage: Cross-filtering and highlighting are interactive features that synchronize data between visuals. When users select data in one visual, other visuals are automatically updated to reflect the selection.

- How to Use: Cross-filtering and highlighting are built into Power BI visuals. You can use these features by setting relationships between tables and visuals.

- Real-time Data Exploration: Users can explore data in real time by selecting data points of interest and seeing how they impact other visuals in the report.

5. Drill-Down:

- Usage: Drill-down allows users to navigate through hierarchical data. For example, users can start with an overview and then drill down into more detailed levels of information.

- How to Use: You can enable drill-down in visuals that support it, such as hierarchy-enabled visuals. Users can expand and collapse levels to navigate through data.

- Visual Hierarchies: Visual hierarchies can be defined in Power BI to support drill-down actions.

6. Tooltip Pages:

- Usage: Tooltip pages provide additional information when users hover over a data point. Tooltips are useful for displaying extra context without cluttering the main report.

- How to Use: You can create tooltip pages in Power BI and define which visuals should display tooltips. Tooltips can include visuals, text, and images.

These interactivity features in Power BI empower users to explore data, gain insights, and make data-driven decisions. When designing reports and dashboards, consider the needs of your audience and how these interactive elements can enhance their experience and understanding of the data. Customizing these features to align with your report's goals and design is essential for creating engaging and informative data visualizations.

Customizing and Branding Reports

Customizing and branding reports in Power BI is a crucial step in creating a professional and cohesive look for your data visualizations. It allows you to tailor the report's appearance to match your organization's branding and create a user-friendly experience. In this section, we'll explore the process of customizing and branding Power BI reports.

1. Choosing a Theme:

- Purpose: Start by selecting an appropriate theme for your report. Power BI offers several built-in themes, and you can create custom themes to match your organization's branding.

- How to Apply: To choose a theme, go to the "View" tab in Power BI Desktop, select "Themes," and apply the desired theme. To create custom themes, you can use the Power BI Theme Generator or manually define JSON files.

2. Adding Logos and Backgrounds:

- Purpose: Incorporate your organization's logo and background images to reinforce branding.

- How to Apply: Go to the "File" menu, select "Options and settings," and then choose "Options." Under "Report settings," you can upload your organization's logo and background image. These images will appear on every page of your report.

3. Color Palette and Fonts:

- Purpose: Define a color palette and font styles that align with your branding.

- How to Apply: In Power BI, you can customize the color palette and font styles under the "View" tab in the "Themes" menu. Use your organization's official colors and fonts to maintain consistency.

4. Formatting Visuals:

- Purpose: Consistent formatting across visuals helps maintain a professional look. You can customize visuals, such as charts and tables, to follow your branding guidelines.

- How to Apply: In Power BI, select a visual and navigate to the "Format" section on the right panel. Here, you can change the colors, fonts, and other formatting options for the selected visual.

5. Custom Page Size and Layout:

- Purpose: You can define custom page sizes and layouts to create unique report structures that match your branding.

- How to Apply: Under the "View" tab in Power BI Desktop, select "Page information" to set custom page sizes. You can also adjust the layout and grid settings to control the placement of visuals.

6. Using Buttons and Bookmarks:

- Purpose: Buttons and bookmarks can be used to create interactive navigation within your report. This can help users explore data more intuitively.

- How to Apply: Design buttons for navigation and create bookmarks to capture specific report states. Set up actions that trigger bookmark changes when users click buttons.

7. Creating a Cover Page:

- Purpose: A cover page introduces your report and provides essential information. It sets the tone for your report's content.

- How to Apply: Create a dedicated cover page in your report that includes a title, date, and summary of the report's purpose. You can use text boxes and visuals to design the cover page.

8. Consistency Across Pages:

- Purpose: Ensure a consistent look and feel throughout your report. Colors, fonts, and other design elements should align with your branding.

- How to Apply: Regularly review and adjust the design elements of your report to maintain consistency. Make use of themes and templates for uniformity.

Customizing and branding your Power BI reports allows you to create an engaging, professional, and consistent user experience. By following the steps above, you can tailor your reports to your organization's identity, making them more visually appealing and easier to navigate. Remember that design is not just about aesthetics but also about usability and effective communication of data insights.

10.2 Real-time Data Insights with Power BI

Implementing Real-time Dashboards

Real-time data insights are crucial in today's fast-paced business environment. Power BI allows you to create interactive and real-time dashboards that provide up-to-the-minute information for making quick, data-driven decisions. In this section, we will explore how to implement real-time dashboards using Power BI.

1. Data Sources for Real-time Dashboards:

- Purpose: To create a real-time dashboard, you need data sources that continuously update, such as IoT devices, log files, or databases with live data feeds.

- How to Implement: Connect to your data source within Power BI. Power BI supports various data connectors, including streaming data sources like Azure Stream Analytics, Power Automate, and custom APIs.

2. Real-time Streaming Setup:

- Purpose: Setting up real-time streaming allows you to keep your dashboard updated as new data arrives.

- How to Implement: Power BI supports real-time streaming datasets. In Power BI Service, go to your workspace, create a streaming dataset, and define data schema. You can use the Power BI REST API or other integration methods to push data to this dataset.

3. Creating Real-time Dashboards:

- Purpose: Design interactive dashboards that update in real-time, displaying the most recent data.

- How to Implement: In Power BI Desktop, add visuals to your report. Utilize streaming visuals (e.g., streaming line chart or real-time data table) for elements that need to update in real-time. Set up automatic refresh for visuals to ensure they display the latest data.

4. Defining Refresh Intervals:

- Purpose: Configure how frequently your visuals should update to match your data source's refresh rate.

- How to Implement: In Power BI Service, navigate to the dataset settings and define the refresh interval. This interval should match the frequency at which your data source sends updates.

5. Real-time Alerts:

- Purpose: Implement alerts to be notified when specific conditions are met in real-time data.

- How to Implement: In Power BI Service, set up alerts based on defined conditions or thresholds. Alerts can trigger emails or push notifications, ensuring you stay informed.

6. Publishing and Sharing:

- Purpose: Share your real-time dashboards with relevant stakeholders.

- How to Implement: Publish your report to Power BI Service, where it can be accessed by team members. Ensure you have configured access and sharing settings appropriately.

7. Mobile Access:

- Purpose: Enable users to access real-time dashboards on mobile devices.

- How to Implement: Power BI offers mobile apps for iOS and Android. Users can access dashboards on their mobile devices to monitor data and receive real-time alerts.

8. Security and Permissions:

- Purpose: Maintain data security and control who can access real-time dashboards.

- How to Implement: Configure security and permissions in Power BI Service to ensure that only authorized users can access sensitive real-time data.

Implementing real-time dashboards with Power BI empowers your organization to make data-driven decisions as events unfold. Whether you're monitoring equipment performance, tracking website traffic, or analyzing financial data, real-time dashboards provide critical insights. By following the steps above, you can design and deploy real-time dashboards that suit your specific business needs and objectives.

Streaming Data Sources and Power BI

Streaming data sources are a critical component when it comes to real-time data insights with Power BI. They allow you to continuously feed fresh data into your reports and dashboards. In this section, we'll delve into the specifics of streaming data sources and how to integrate them with Power BI.

1. Choose the Appropriate Streaming Data Source:

- Purpose: The first step is to identify and choose the right streaming data source for your scenario. Streaming data sources are typically sources that produce continuous data, such as IoT devices, social media feeds, or real-time application logs.

- How to Implement: Connect to the chosen streaming data source. Power BI supports various connectors for streaming data, including Azure Stream Analytics, Power Automate, and custom APIs.

2. Data Transformation and Enrichment:

- Purpose: To ensure your streaming data is in a suitable format and enriched with relevant information before being used in Power BI.

- How to Implement: You may need to use tools and services like Azure Functions, Azure Databricks, or Stream Analytics to transform and enrich your streaming data. This step ensures that the data fits your reporting requirements.

3. Creating a Streaming Dataset:

- Purpose: Setting up a streaming dataset in Power BI Service allows you to receive and visualize real-time data.

- How to Implement: In Power BI Service, navigate to your workspace, create a streaming dataset, and define the schema of your data. This step defines how incoming data should be structured and visualized.

4. Data Push Mechanism:

- Purpose: Determine how data will be pushed from your streaming source to Power BI.

- How to Implement: You can use Power BI's REST API or other integration methods to push data to the streaming dataset. Some data sources may have built-in connectors for Power BI.

5. Defining Real-time Data Update Intervals:

- Purpose: Configure the refresh intervals for your streaming dataset to match the frequency at which your data source produces data.

- How to Implement: In Power BI Service, you can set the refresh intervals for your streaming dataset. This setting ensures that your real-time data updates align with your data source's pace.

6. Visualizing Streaming Data:

- Purpose: Use Power BI visuals to display and analyze the incoming streaming data.

- How to Implement: In Power BI Desktop, add streaming visuals (e.g., streaming line chart or real-time data table) to your report. These visuals are designed to update in real-time and display the most recent data.

7. Security and Permissions:

- Purpose: Ensure data security and manage who can access and modify streaming datasets.

- How to Implement: Configure security and permissions for your streaming dataset in Power BI Service. This step is crucial to protect sensitive real-time data.

By integrating streaming data sources with Power BI, you can create real-time dashboards and reports that offer immediate insights into dynamic data. Whether you're monitoring social media trends, tracking sensor data from IoT devices, or keeping an eye on web traffic, streaming data sources empower your organization to respond to events as they happen. Follow the above steps to effectively connect and visualize streaming data with Power BI.

Monitoring Data and Triggering Alerts in Real-time

Monitoring your real-time data is crucial for staying informed about important events and changes as they happen. Power BI offers features for monitoring data and triggering alerts in real-time, allowing you to react promptly to evolving situations.

1. Setting Up Data Alerts:

- Purpose: Data alerts notify you when specific conditions in your data are met, providing real-time insights.

- How to Implement:

  - In Power BI Service, open the report or dashboard you want to monitor.

  - Select a visual or element you want to set an alert for.

  - Click on the "More options" (represented by three dots) in the visual's top right corner.

  - Choose "Set alert" and configure your alert conditions.

  - Specify alert recipients, delivery methods (e.g., email or mobile notifications), and frequency.

2. Using Streaming Data for Alerts:

- Purpose: You can leverage streaming datasets and real-time data for setting up alerts.

- How to Implement:

  - Connect your real-time data source to a streaming dataset, as described in the previous section.

  - Create alerts based on data conditions from the streaming dataset.

  - Configure the alerts to trigger when certain thresholds are met.

3. Real-time Data Integration:

- Purpose: To keep your data monitoring and alerting in sync with the real-time nature of your data sources.

- How to Implement: Make sure that your data alerts are configured with short refresh intervals that match your streaming data's update frequency. This ensures that alerts are triggered as soon as new data is available.

4. Common Alert Scenarios:

- Purpose: Real-time data monitoring is useful for a wide range of scenarios.

- How to Implement:

  - For IoT applications, set up alerts for sensor readings that cross predefined thresholds.

  - In financial services, monitor stock prices and currencies for sudden changes.

  - In e-commerce, track website traffic and sales figures, and trigger alerts for unusual spikes or drops.

  - In social media analysis, get alerts when a particular hashtag or keyword trends.

5. Response Mechanisms:

- Purpose: Determine the actions to be taken when alerts are triggered.

- How to Implement: Define clear and appropriate actions for each type of alert. These actions may include manual intervention, sending notifications to designated teams, or executing automated responses via Power Automate or other integrations.

6. Alert Logging and Reporting:

- Purpose: Maintain a record of alerts and responses for compliance and analysis.

- How to Implement: Keep a log of all alerts triggered and responses taken. Power BI offers options for storing alert history and generating reports to track alert trends and effectiveness.

7. Testing and Fine-Tuning:

- Purpose: Continuously improve your alerts by testing and adjusting their thresholds.

- How to Implement: Regularly review the effectiveness of your alerts. Modify conditions and responses based on feedback and changing data patterns.

By implementing real-time monitoring and data alerts in Power BI, you can stay informed and take swift actions when important events occur. Whether it's tracking business metrics, monitoring IoT devices, or keeping an eye on social media trends, real-time alerts are a valuable tool for data-driven decision-making. Follow these steps to set up effective alerts and maximize the benefits of your real-time data insights.

CHAPTER X
Managing and Maintaining Power BI and Azure Solutions

11.1 Deployment and Updates

Managing Power BI Workspaces

In Power BI, workspaces play a crucial role in organizing and managing your reports, dashboards, and datasets. Effectively managing Power BI workspaces is essential for collaboration and ensuring that your business intelligence solutions run smoothly. Here, we will explore the best practices for managing Power BI workspaces:

1. Creating Workspaces:

   - Purpose: Create workspaces to logically group related reports and dashboards, making it easier for teams to collaborate and manage content.

   - How to Implement:

     - In Power BI Service, go to your workspace area.

     - Click "Create a workspace" and provide a name and optional description.

     - You can set the workspace as "My workspace" or create a shared workspace for your team.

2. Workspace Naming Conventions:

   - Purpose: Establish consistent naming conventions for workspaces to maintain clarity.

   - How to Implement:

- Use descriptive names that reflect the workspace's content or department.

- Consider using abbreviations or codes for uniformity.

3. Managing Permissions:

- Purpose: Control who can access and edit the content within a workspace.

- How to Implement:

- Share workspaces with specific users or groups and define their access levels (Admin, Member, Contributor, or Viewer).

- Regularly review and update permissions as team membership changes.

4. Content Organization:

- Purpose: Keep content well-organized within workspaces for easy navigation.

- How to Implement:

- Use folders within workspaces to group related reports, dashboards, and datasets.

- Create a folder structure that reflects the logical organization of your business.

5. Workspace Usage Metrics:

- Purpose: Monitor the usage of each workspace to understand which reports and dashboards are most popular.

- How to Implement:

- Power BI provides usage metrics for each workspace, including views, interactions, and more.

- Use these metrics to assess content engagement and make data-driven decisions.

6. Managing Workspace Members:

- Purpose: Ensure the right people have access to workspaces and their content.

- How to Implement:

  - Add or remove members as team composition changes.

  - Communicate with members about workspace changes and updates.

7. Workspace Settings and Configuration:

  - Purpose: Configure workspace settings to align with your organization's requirements.

  - How to Implement:

    - Adjust settings like export and data refresh options.

    - Set up dataflows and shared datasets if needed.

8. Workspace Archiving and Cleanup:

  - Purpose: Maintain a clean workspace environment by archiving or deleting obsolete workspaces and content.

  - How to Implement:

    - Archive workspaces that are no longer in active use but may contain valuable historical data.

    - Ensure you have a backup or export of any important content before deleting workspaces.

9. Communication and Documentation:

  - Purpose: Keep team members informed about changes and developments in workspaces.

  - How to Implement:

    - Use collaboration tools and maintain documentation to explain workspace organization, permissions, and data sources.

10. Training and Onboarding:

  - Purpose: Ensure that all workspace members are well-trained on Power BI and understand workspace-related processes.

- How to Implement:

  - Provide training sessions and resources for new members to familiarize them with workspace management practices.

Effective management of Power BI workspaces is vital for maintaining a streamlined and collaborative environment. With these practices, you can ensure that your teams work efficiently and can quickly access the reports and dashboards they need for data-driven decision-making. Regularly review and update your workspace management procedures to adapt to changing business requirements and team dynamics.

Automated Deployment Strategies

Automated deployment strategies in Power BI and Azure are crucial for ensuring the smooth and efficient rollout of reports, dashboards, and data solutions. Automation reduces the risk of errors, enhances productivity, and allows teams to focus on data analysis and insights. In this section, we'll explore the strategies and best practices for automated deployments:

1. Version Control:

   - Purpose: Maintain a central repository of your Power BI reports and datasets.

   - How to Implement:

     - Use version control systems like Git to store Power BI files (PBIX), DAX scripts, and data source connection details.

     - Collaborate with team members, enabling efficient change tracking and sharing of PBIX files.

2. Continuous Integration (CI):

   - Purpose: Automate the process of merging code changes and datasets.

   - How to Implement:

- Utilize CI pipelines in Azure DevOps, GitHub Actions, or other CI/CD tools to merge code and data updates.

- Automate data refreshes, allowing datasets to be updated regularly.

3. Dev, Test, and Production Environments:

  - Purpose: Separate your deployment process into development, testing, and production stages.

  - How to Implement:

  - Create distinct workspaces in Power BI for development, testing, and production.

  - Develop and test reports and dashboards in the appropriate environment before promoting them to production.

4. Deployment Automation Scripts:

  - Purpose: Write scripts to automate deployment tasks.

  - How to Implement:

  - Create PowerShell or Python scripts that handle tasks such as publishing reports to Power BI Service, configuring data source connections, and refreshing datasets.

  - Use Power BI REST APIs to automate interactions with Power BI Service.

5. Azure Resource Manager (ARM) Templates:

  - Purpose: Deploy and manage Azure resources alongside Power BI reports.

  - How to Implement:

  - Use ARM templates to define and deploy Azure resources like Azure SQL Databases, Azure Data Factories, or Azure Analysis Services.

  - Combine ARM templates with Power BI deployment scripts for end-to-end automation.

6. Scheduled Deployments:

- Purpose: Automate deployment schedules to avoid manual intervention.

- How to Implement:

  - Schedule automated deployments during non-business hours to minimize disruptions.

  - Consider using triggers in CI/CD pipelines for on-demand deployments.

7. Error Handling and Rollbacks:

  - Purpose: Implement error-handling procedures and rollback mechanisms in case of deployment issues.

  - How to Implement:

    - Monitor deployments for errors and set up alerts to notify responsible personnel.

    - Develop scripts or processes to quickly revert to the previous working state in case of issues.

8. Documentation and Reporting:

  - Purpose: Maintain documentation for deployment processes and history.

  - How to Implement:

    - Document the steps for each deployment process and make them accessible to the team.

    - Generate reports or logs of each deployment, including timestamps, changes, and success/failure status.

9. Regular Testing:

  - Purpose: Continuously test deployment processes to ensure they remain effective.

  - How to Implement:

    - Implement automated testing for deployment scripts and processes.

    - Conduct periodic reviews of deployment procedures to identify and address any improvements or changes needed.

10. Security and Access Control:

  - Purpose: Ensure that access to deployment scripts and processes is controlled.

  - How to Implement:

    - Restrict access to deployment scripts and automation tools to authorized team members.

    - Follow best practices for securing credentials and sensitive information used in deployment scripts.

Automated deployment strategies are essential for maintaining a stable and efficient Power BI and Azure environment. By following these best practices and leveraging automation tools, your team can reduce manual errors, enhance collaboration, and ensure that reports, dashboards, and datasets are reliably deployed and updated.

Updating Reports and Dashboards

Keeping your Power BI reports and dashboards up to date is crucial for providing accurate and relevant insights to your organization. In this section, we'll explore the best practices for updating reports and dashboards effectively:

1. Data Source Refresh:

  - Purpose: Ensure that your reports reflect the latest data.

  - How to Implement:

    - Set up scheduled data refresh in Power BI Service to automatically update datasets.

    - Configure data source connections, credentials, and gateway settings.

2. Report Publishing:

  - Purpose: Publish updated reports to Power BI Service.

  - How to Implement:

- Use Power BI Desktop to make changes and enhancements to reports.

- Publish the updated reports to the appropriate workspace in Power BI Service.

3. Version Control:

  - Purpose: Maintain version control for your reports.

  - How to Implement:

    - Use version control systems like Git to track changes to your Power BI files (PBIX).

    - Implement branching and merging strategies for collaborative development.

4. Incremental Loading:

  - Purpose: Optimize data loading for large datasets.

  - How to Implement:

    - Implement incremental loading to load only new or changed data.

    - Utilize Power Query or DAX for creating incremental load scripts.

5. Data Transformation:

  - Purpose: Transform data to match evolving business requirements.

  - How to Implement:

    - Use Power Query in Power BI Desktop for data transformation.

    - Maintain clear documentation of data transformations and logic.

6. Data Validation:

  - Purpose: Verify the accuracy and integrity of updated data.

  - How to Implement:

    - Implement data validation checks to ensure data consistency.

- Schedule automated tests or use data profiling tools.

7. Monitoring and Alerts:

  - Purpose: Monitor reports and dashboards for issues.

  - How to Implement:

    - Set up alerts in Power BI Service to notify stakeholders of report failures or anomalies.

    - Establish a monitoring process to track the performance of reports.

8. Documentation:

  - Purpose: Maintain documentation of report updates.

  - How to Implement:

    - Document changes made to reports, including the reason for the update.

    - Use a change log or documentation tool to track report revisions.

9. Versioning of Reports:

  - Purpose: Track and manage different report versions.

  - How to Implement:

    - Maintain multiple report versions in Power BI Service workspaces.

    - Clearly label and document different versions for easy reference.

10. User Training and Communication:

  - Purpose: Ensure users are informed of report updates.

  - How to Implement:

    - Communicate changes to users through training sessions or documentation.

    - Collect feedback and provide support for any questions or issues.

11. Rollback Plan:

  - Purpose: Prepare for potential issues in the update process.

  - How to Implement:

    - Create a rollback plan that outlines steps to revert to the previous version in case of problems.

    - Test the rollback process to ensure its effectiveness.

12. User Acceptance Testing (UAT):

  - Purpose: Involve end-users in testing updated reports.

  - How to Implement:

    - Conduct UAT to ensure that the updated reports meet user expectations and requirements.

    - Collect feedback from UAT and address any identified issues.

Updating reports and dashboards in Power BI requires a well-defined process to maintain data accuracy and ensure that stakeholders have access to the latest insights. By following these best practices, your organization can keep reports up to date and support informed decision-making.

11.2 Backup and Recovery Strategies

Data Backup in Azure

Data backup is a critical component of ensuring the availability and integrity of your data in Azure. Azure provides several services and strategies for backing up your data, ensuring you can recover it in case of accidental deletion, data corruption, or other disasters. In this section, we will delve into data backup strategies in Azure.

1. Azure Backup Service:

   - Purpose: Azure Backup is a fully managed cloud backup service that simplifies data protection.

   - How to Implement:

     - In the Azure portal, create a Recovery Services vault.

     - Configure a backup policy that specifies what to back up and how often.

     - Assign the policy to the target resources (e.g., virtual machines, databases).

2. Blob Storage Backup:

   - Purpose: Back up data stored in Azure Blob Storage.

   - How to Implement:

     - Use Azure Blob Storage lifecycle management to create backups of your data.

     - Define policies for transitioning data to a backup storage tier.

3. Database Backup:

   - Purpose: Protect your databases in Azure.

- How to Implement:

  - For Azure SQL Database, use automated database backups that are retained for a specified period.

  - For virtual machines running database software, configure database-specific backup solutions.

4. Azure Site Recovery:

  - Purpose: Ensure business continuity with disaster recovery.

  - How to Implement:

    - Set up Azure Site Recovery to replicate virtual machines to a secondary Azure region.

    - Define recovery plans to orchestrate the failover and failback processes.

5. Azure File Sync:

  - Purpose: Synchronize file servers and back up data to Azure Files.

  - How to Implement:

    - Deploy Azure File Sync on your on-premises file servers.

    - Configure synchronization and backup settings.

6. Managed Disk Snapshots:

  - Purpose: Create point-in-time backups of managed disks.

  - How to Implement:

    - Use Azure Managed Disks to create snapshots of disks attached to virtual machines.

    - Configure snapshot retention policies.

7. Azure Policy and Blueprints:

  - Purpose: Enforce backup and data protection policies across your organization.

  - How to Implement:

    - Define Azure Policy or Blueprints that enforce backup requirements.

    - Apply these policies to Azure subscriptions or resource groups.

8. Data Encryption and Key Management:

  - Purpose: Protect your backup data with encryption.

  - How to Implement:

    - Use Azure Key Vault to manage encryption keys for backup data.

    - Enable encryption for backup services and storage.

9. Monitoring and Alerting:

  - Purpose: Ensure that backups are running as expected.

  - How to Implement:

    - Set up monitoring and alerting for Azure Backup jobs.

    - Use Azure Monitor and Application Insights to gain visibility into backup operations.

10. Testing and Recovery Drills:

  - Purpose: Validate the effectiveness of your backup and recovery strategies.

  - How to Implement:

    - Regularly conduct recovery drills to test your backup and recovery processes.

    - Document and analyze the results of these drills to make improvements.

Data backup is a fundamental part of your disaster recovery and business continuity planning. With Azure's backup services and strategies, you can ensure the safety and recoverability of your data, whether it's stored in virtual machines, databases, or file servers. By implementing these backup practices, you can protect your organization from data loss and downtime.

Disaster Recovery Planning

Disaster recovery planning is a crucial aspect of ensuring business continuity and data protection in Azure. This section covers the key components and steps involved in effective disaster recovery planning.

1. Risk Assessment:

  - Purpose: Identify potential risks and threats to your Azure resources.

  - How to Implement:

   - Conduct a risk assessment that considers natural disasters, human errors, cyberattacks, and other potential threats.

   - Prioritize these risks based on their potential impact and likelihood.

2. Define Recovery Objectives:

  - Purpose: Determine the recovery time objective (RTO) and recovery point objective (RPO) for your Azure resources.

  - How to Implement:

   - Set clear objectives for how quickly you need to recover your systems (RTO) and how much data loss is acceptable (RPO).

3. Backup and Replication Strategy:

- Purpose: Choose the appropriate backup and replication strategies to meet your recovery objectives.

- How to Implement:

- Decide which Azure services (e.g., Azure Backup, Azure Site Recovery) you will use for backup and replication.

- Configure these services to align with your RTO and RPO goals.

4. Disaster Recovery Runbooks:

- Purpose: Document the procedures and workflows for disaster recovery.

- How to Implement:

- Create detailed runbooks that outline the steps for recovering specific resources or services.

- Ensure these runbooks are easily accessible to your recovery team.

5. Cross-Region Replication:

- Purpose: Replicate your Azure resources to a secondary Azure region.

- How to Implement:

- Set up Azure Site Recovery to replicate virtual machines, databases, and other resources to a secondary Azure region.

- Define failover plans to facilitate the recovery process.

6. Data Recovery and Testing:

- Purpose: Regularly test your disaster recovery plans and verify data recoverability.

- How to Implement:

- Schedule and perform disaster recovery tests to ensure that your recovery procedures are effective.

- Document the results of these tests and make improvements as needed.

7. Azure Policy and Compliance:

- Purpose: Ensure that your disaster recovery plans align with Azure policies and compliance standards.

- How to Implement:

- Enforce compliance with Azure Policy and implement specific policies related to disaster recovery.

- Regularly review and update your disaster recovery policies to stay compliant.

8. Monitoring and Alerting:

- Purpose: Continuously monitor the health of your Azure resources and trigger alerts for potential issues.

- How to Implement:

- Set up monitoring solutions to track the performance and availability of Azure services.

- Configure alerts to be notified of any deviations from normal operation.

9. Documentation and Training:

- Purpose: Ensure that your recovery team is well-prepared and informed about disaster recovery procedures.

- How to Implement:

- Provide comprehensive documentation and training to your recovery team.

- Conduct regular training sessions to keep your team up to date.

10. Communication Plan:

- Purpose: Establish a clear communication plan for notifying stakeholders during a disaster.

- How to Implement:

- Create a communication plan that defines how and when to inform relevant parties about a disaster event.

- Test your communication plan to ensure its effectiveness.

Disaster recovery planning is essential for minimizing downtime and data loss during unexpected events. By following these steps and best practices, you can create a robust disaster recovery plan that aligns with your business objectives and ensures the continuity of your Azure solutions.

Backup and Restore in Power BI

Power BI offers various methods for backing up and restoring your reports, datasets, and dashboards to protect your data and ensure business continuity. In this section, we'll explore the backup and restore procedures in Power BI.

1. Automated Backups in Power BI Service:

- Purpose: Automatically back up your datasets and reports in the Power BI service.

- How to Implement:

- Power BI offers an automated backup feature that enables you to create regular backups of your datasets and reports.

- Configure backup settings, including the frequency and retention policy for backups.

2. Manual Backup Using Export:

- Purpose: Manually export reports, datasets, and dashboards for backup purposes.

- How to Implement:

- In the Power BI service, you can manually export your reports and datasets by selecting the content you want to export.

- Exported files can be stored in a secure location for backup and recovery.

3. Power BI Paginated Reports:

- Purpose: Back up paginated reports for additional report types.

- How to Implement:

- Paginated reports are exportable to formats like PDF, Excel, and more.

- Regularly export and store paginated reports for backup.

4. Power BI Dataflows:

- Purpose: Backup Power BI dataflows, which store and transform data.

- How to Implement:

- Power BI dataflows can be manually exported or included in automated backups.

5. Using Power BI Gateway:

- Purpose: Backup datasets by configuring the Power BI Gateway.

- How to Implement:

- Data from on-premises data sources can be refreshed and backed up using the Power BI Gateway.

- Set up gateways to ensure data continuity.

6. Workspace Settings:

- Purpose: Configure workspace settings to enforce backup and retention policies.

- How to Implement:

   - Within your workspaces, define policies related to backup and retention.

7. Recovery in Power BI Service:

   - Purpose: Restore content from backups as needed.

   - How to Implement:

   - When data loss occurs, you can initiate a recovery process in the Power BI service to restore content from your backups.

8. PowerShell Scripts:

   - Purpose: Use PowerShell scripts to automate backup and restore operations.

   - How to Implement:

   - Develop PowerShell scripts that interact with Power BI REST APIs to automate backup and restore processes.

   - This is particularly useful for large-scale or scheduled operations.

9. Considerations for Data Loss Prevention:

   - Purpose: Implement data loss prevention strategies to prevent accidental data loss.

   - How to Implement:

   - Establish policies and educate your team about data loss prevention best practices.

   - Implement role-based access controls and monitoring to avoid data loss incidents.

Power BI offers flexibility in backup and recovery options to meet your specific needs. Whether you prefer automated backups, manual exports, or a combination of both, it's essential to regularly back up your critical Power BI content to ensure data protection and continuity. Be prepared to initiate recovery processes as needed to minimize downtime in case of data loss or disasters.

11.3 Troubleshooting Common Issues

Diagnosing Data Connection Problems

Ensuring a reliable data connection is crucial for successful data analysis and reporting in Power BI. When you encounter data connection problems, it's essential to diagnose and resolve these issues promptly. In this section, we will explore the common steps to diagnose data connection problems in Power BI:

1. Verify Data Source Credentials:

   - Purpose: Ensure that the credentials used to connect to your data source are correct.

   - How to Diagnose:

     - Check the username, password, and any other necessary authentication details.

     - Test the credentials outside of Power BI, such as in SQL Server Management Studio or the data source's web interface.

2. Check Data Source Availability:

   - Purpose: Confirm that the data source is available and accessible.

   - How to Diagnose:

     - Verify that the data source server is running and reachable.

     - Check network connectivity to the data source.

3. Validate Data Source URLs:

   - Purpose: Ensure that the URLs or connection strings used to access the data source are correct.

   - How to Diagnose:

- Review the URLs, paths, and connection strings in your data source settings.

- Correct any inaccuracies or typographical errors.

4. Test Query Execution:

  - Purpose: Examine the execution of queries to identify issues.

  - How to Diagnose:

    - Use query tools within Power BI, such as Power Query Editor, to run and debug queries.

    - Pay attention to error messages, which can pinpoint the problem.

5. Connection and Timeout Settings:

  - Purpose: Adjust connection and timeout settings as needed.

  - How to Diagnose:

    - Review and modify settings such as connection timeout, query timeout, and maximum connections.

    - Ensure that these settings align with your data source requirements.

6. Query Folding and Data Privacy:

  - Purpose: Understand query folding and data privacy settings.

  - How to Diagnose:

    - Investigate whether query folding is occurring. Query folding can optimize data retrieval.

    - Evaluate data privacy settings to ensure data is handled appropriately.

7. Query Performance Profiling:

  - Purpose: Profile query performance to identify bottlenecks.

- How to Diagnose:

  - Use the Query Diagnostics feature in Power BI to analyze query performance.

  - Identify slow queries, data shaping issues, and query folding behavior.

8. Data Source Documentation:

  - Purpose: Maintain documentation for your data sources.

  - How to Diagnose:

  - Create and maintain documentation that includes data source details, connection information, and query examples.

  - Documentation assists in diagnosing and resolving issues efficiently.

9. Community and Support Resources:

  - Purpose: Leverage community forums and official support channels.

  - How to Diagnose:

  - If issues persist, seek guidance and solutions from the Power BI community and official support resources.

  - Forums and support can provide valuable insights into resolving complex problems.

10. Data Source-Specific Troubleshooting:

  - Purpose: Learn about common issues and resolutions specific to your data source.

  - How to Diagnose:

  - Consult data source-specific documentation and resources for troubleshooting guidance.

  - Different data sources may have unique issues and solutions.

Diagnosing data connection problems requires a methodical approach, including verifying credentials, assessing data source availability, testing queries, and adjusting settings as needed. By following these steps and relying on community support when necessary, you can resolve data connection issues and ensure the reliability of your Power BI reports and dashboards.

Debugging Performance Issues

Optimizing the performance of your Power BI reports and dashboards is essential to ensure a smooth and responsive user experience. When you encounter performance issues, it's crucial to identify and address the root causes. In this section, we will explore the common steps to debug performance issues in Power BI:

1. Identify Performance Bottlenecks:

   - Purpose: Determine which parts of your report are causing performance issues.

   - How to Debug:

   - Use the Performance Analyzer tool in Power BI to identify slow-performing visuals, DAX calculations, or data queries.

   - Pay attention to visuals with long rendering times.

2. Optimize Data Queries:

   - Purpose: Optimize the queries that retrieve data from your data source.

   - How to Debug:

   - Use Power Query Editor to review and optimize data retrieval queries.

   - Ensure that you're retrieving only the necessary data.

   - Check for inefficient joins, transformations, and filtering steps.

3. Use Query Folding:

   - Purpose: Ensure that query folding is occurring for supported data sources.

   - How to Debug:

     - Review query execution plans to verify whether query folding is taking place.

     - Modify queries or data source settings to enable query folding where possible.

4. Optimize Data Model:

   - Purpose: Improve the data model's efficiency.

   - How to Debug:

     - Evaluate your data model's structure and relationships. Simplify if necessary.

     - Remove unnecessary calculated columns or measures.

     - Avoid using large, unaggregated tables in visuals.

5. DAX Optimization:

   - Purpose: Optimize Data Analysis Expressions (DAX) calculations.

   - How to Debug:

     - Use DAX Studio to profile and optimize DAX calculations.

     - Identify and refactor complex or inefficient DAX expressions.

     - Consider using calculated tables instead of calculated columns for certain scenarios.

6. Visual-Level Optimization:

   - Purpose: Optimize individual visuals.

   - How to Debug:

- Adjust visual-level filters, cross-filtering behavior, and interactions.

- Minimize the use of visuals that require extensive processing, such as tables with many rows.

7. Aggregation and Summary Tables:

   - Purpose: Use aggregations and summary tables for large datasets.

   - How to Debug:

     - Create aggregations to pre-calculate summary values for large fact tables.

     - Link aggregations to visuals that require them.

8. Enable Load on Demand:

   - Purpose: Optimize report performance by enabling load-on-demand for visuals.

   - How to Debug:

     - Configure visuals to load data only when the user interacts with them.

     - Avoid loading all data upfront.

9. Performance Profiling:

   - Purpose: Use the built-in Performance Analyzer in Power BI.

   - How to Debug:

     - Profile report performance to identify bottlenecks.

     - Analyze the time taken by visuals, DAX calculations, and data queries.

10. Hardware and Infrastructure:

   - Purpose: Assess the hardware and infrastructure used for Power BI.

- How to Debug:

  - Ensure that the hardware and network infrastructure can support the required performance.

  - Monitor system resources on the Power BI service for cloud-based reports.

11. Collaboration and Testing:

  - Purpose: Collaborate with users and testers to gather feedback.

  - How to Debug:

    - Involve end-users in testing and optimizing report performance.

    - Use feedback to refine and improve the report's performance.

Debugging performance issues in Power BI involves identifying bottlenecks, optimizing data queries, refining the data model, and streamlining DAX calculations. By following these steps and leveraging performance profiling tools, you can ensure that your reports and dashboards deliver a responsive and efficient user experience.

Handling Security and Access Problems

Ensuring that your Power BI reports and dashboards are secure and that access is properly managed is a critical aspect of managing your solutions. Security and access problems can arise for various reasons, and addressing them promptly is essential. In this section, we will explore common security and access issues and how to handle them:

1. Data Source Permissions:

  - Issue: Users are unable to access data sources or are experiencing permission-related errors.

  - Resolution:

- Review and adjust data source permissions in your data source platform (e.g., Azure SQL Database, SharePoint, or on-premises sources).

- Ensure that users have the necessary permissions to access the underlying data.

2. Power BI Service Permissions:

- Issue: Users encounter issues with accessing reports or dashboards in the Power BI Service.

- Resolution:

- Check user roles and permissions within the Power BI Service. Assign the appropriate roles to users, such as members or administrators.

- Ensure that content is shared with the intended users or groups.

3. Row-Level Security:

- Issue: Certain users are seeing data they shouldn't have access to.

- Resolution:

- Implement row-level security in Power BI to restrict data access based on user roles.

- Verify that the security filters and rules are correctly configured.

4. Single Sign-On (SSO) and Authentication:

- Issue: Users face authentication or SSO issues when accessing reports.

- Resolution:

- Review and configure authentication settings, including SSO, in your organization's Power BI settings.

- Verify that authentication providers, such as Azure Active Directory, are properly configured.

5. Data Encryption:

  - Issue: Concerns about data security and encryption.

  - Resolution:

    - Ensure that data connections between Power BI and data sources are encrypted.

    - Implement encryption for data at rest where required.

6. Access Revocation:

  - Issue: Need to revoke access for specific users or groups.

  - Resolution:

    - Revoke access at both the data source level and Power BI Service.

    - Ensure that sensitive data remains secure when access is revoked.

7. Audit and Monitoring:

  - Issue: Lack of visibility into who accesses what data.

  - Resolution:

    - Configure audit and monitoring features in the Power BI Service and data source platforms.

    - Regularly review audit logs to identify suspicious activities.

8. Content Lifecycle Management:

  - Issue: Stale or outdated content remains accessible.

  - Resolution:

    - Implement content lifecycle management policies to archive or remove outdated content.

    - Define procedures for reviewing and retiring old reports and dashboards.

9. Training and Awareness:

  - Issue: Users are unaware of security best practices.

  - Resolution:

   - Provide training and resources to educate users about security best practices in Power BI.

   - Encourage users to report security concerns promptly.

Handling security and access problems requires a proactive approach to managing permissions, access controls, and authentication settings. Regularly monitor and audit your Power BI environment to ensure data security and compliance with your organization's policies. Additionally, educating users about security best practices is crucial for maintaining a secure environment.

CHAPTER XI
Data Governance and Compliance

12.1 Data Governance Best Practices

Establishing Data Governance Policies

Data governance is crucial for ensuring that data is managed, used, and protected effectively within an organization. Establishing data governance policies helps define the rules and procedures for handling data throughout its lifecycle. In this section, we will explore best practices for establishing data governance policies:

1. Define Data Governance Objectives:

   - Clearly articulate the goals and objectives of your data governance policies. Understand what you aim to achieve, such as data security, compliance, data quality, or data access management.

2. Identify Stakeholders:

   - Determine who within your organization is responsible for data governance. This may include data stewards, data owners, compliance officers, and IT personnel.

3. Data Classification:

   - Implement a data classification system to categorize data based on its sensitivity and criticality. This classification helps determine how data should be handled and protected.

4. Data Ownership:

   - Assign data ownership to individuals or teams. Data owners are responsible for making decisions about data access, changes, and overall data management.

5. Data Policies and Procedures:

   - Develop clear and comprehensive data policies and procedures. These should cover data retention, access control, data quality standards, and data sharing guidelines.

6. Compliance Requirements:

   - Ensure that data governance policies align with legal and regulatory compliance requirements specific to your industry. This includes GDPR, HIPAA, or other data protection regulations.

7. Metadata Management:

   - Establish metadata management practices to catalog and document data assets. Metadata should include information about data lineage, data sources, and data definitions.

8. Data Quality Standards:

   - Define data quality standards and metrics. Regularly monitor data quality and implement processes for data cleansing and validation.

9. Access Control and Authentication:

   - Implement access control measures to restrict data access based on user roles and permissions. Ensure that authentication mechanisms are robust.

10. Data Privacy and Security:

- Set guidelines for data privacy and security. This includes encryption, data masking, and securing data at rest and in transit.

11. Communication and Training:

- Communicate data governance policies across the organization. Provide training to employees to ensure they understand and follow these policies.

12. Data Governance Tools:

- Utilize data governance tools and platforms to help automate and enforce policies. These tools can assist with data cataloging, lineage tracking, and compliance monitoring.

13. Regular Auditing and Monitoring:

- Continuously audit and monitor data governance practices to ensure compliance and identify areas for improvement. Regularly update policies as needed.

14. Data Governance Committee:

- Consider establishing a data governance committee responsible for overseeing and enforcing data governance policies.

Data governance policies should be adaptable to your organization's needs and evolve as data-related challenges change. Establishing these policies is the first step toward effective data governance, ensuring that data is an asset rather than a liability for your organization.

Data Catalogs and Metadata Management

Data catalogs and metadata management are critical components of effective data governance and compliance. A data catalog acts as a centralized repository that organizes, documents, and indexes metadata related to your organization's data assets. Metadata provides valuable information about data, such as its source, structure, lineage, and usage. In this section, we will explore best practices for managing data catalogs and metadata:

1. Data Catalog Creation:

   - Choose a data cataloging tool or platform (e.g., Azure Data Catalog, Collibra, Apache Atlas) to create a centralized repository for metadata. Ensure it supports a wide range of data sources.

2. Metadata Types:

   - Define metadata types that are relevant to your organization. Common metadata types include technical metadata (e.g., data source, schema), business metadata (e.g., data definitions, business rules), and operational metadata (e.g., data access history).

3. Data Asset Profiling:

   - Profile data assets to automatically extract technical metadata, such as data types, column names, and data distribution. This can save time and ensure consistency in metadata.

4. Data Lineage Tracking:

   - Implement data lineage tracking to understand how data flows from source to destination. Document transformations, data integration points, and any data movements between systems.

5. Data Definitions and Business Glossary:

   - Create a business glossary that defines common business terms and their meanings. Associate these definitions with data elements to ensure a shared understanding of data.

6. Data Ownership:

   - Assign data ownership to individuals or teams. Data owners are responsible for maintaining metadata accuracy and ensuring data governance policies are followed.

7. Metadata Governance Policies:

- Develop policies and procedures for managing metadata. Define who can edit metadata, what changes are allowed, and how metadata should be validated.

8. Data Catalog User Access:

- Implement role-based access control to ensure that only authorized users can view, edit, or add metadata. Different roles may include data stewards, data owners, and data consumers.

9. Automated Metadata Capture:

- Implement automated mechanisms for capturing metadata whenever new data assets are ingested or changes occur. Automation reduces the risk of manual errors.

10. Data Quality and Consistency:

- Ensure that metadata is consistent and accurate. Establish data quality standards for metadata, and regularly audit metadata for inconsistencies.

11. Search and Discovery:

- Enable a robust search and discovery interface within the data catalog. Users should be able to find data assets and associated metadata quickly.

12. Data Lineage Visualization:

- Use visualization tools to present data lineage in a clear and understandable manner. Visualizations help users track data transformations.

13. Integration with Data Governance Tools:

- Integrate your data catalog with other data governance tools to enforce data policies, compliance, and data security.

14. Metadata Training:

   - Provide training for employees to understand the importance of metadata and how to work with the data catalog. Encourage a metadata-aware culture within your organization.

Effective data cataloging and metadata management help maintain data quality, improve data discoverability, and facilitate compliance. As data assets grow, having a well-managed data catalog becomes increasingly essential for organizations to gain valuable insights from their data while adhering to governance and compliance requirements.

Data Quality and Data Lineage

Data quality and data lineage are vital components of effective data governance and compliance. In this section, we will delve into best practices for managing data quality and data lineage to ensure data is accurate, trustworthy, and compliant:

Data Quality:

1. Data Quality Framework: Develop a data quality framework that defines data quality standards, metrics, and expectations for your organization. This framework should encompass aspects like accuracy, completeness, consistency, and reliability.

2. Data Profiling: Use data profiling tools to assess the quality of your data. These tools can identify data anomalies, missing values, and inconsistencies.

3. Data Quality Assessment: Regularly assess and monitor data quality. Create data quality scorecards and reports to track the health of your data.

4. Data Quality Rules: Define data quality rules and constraints to enforce standards and flag data issues. Automated checks should be integrated into data processing workflows.

5. Data Cleansing: Implement data cleansing processes to correct or remove erroneous data. Develop strategies to handle missing data or outliers.

6. Data Validation: Validate data at various stages of data processing, including data ingestion, transformation, and reporting. Automated data validation checks should be part of your data pipeline.

7. Data Stewardship: Appoint data stewards responsible for data quality in their respective domains. Data stewards should resolve data quality issues and ensure adherence to data quality rules.

8. Data Profiling Tools: Utilize data profiling tools that can automatically identify data anomalies and assist data stewards in data quality management.

Data Lineage:

9. Data Lineage Capture: Implement data lineage tracking to record the flow of data from source to destination. Document transformations, data integration points, and any data movements between systems.

10. Metadata Integration: Integrate data lineage information into your data catalog and metadata management system. This provides a holistic view of data assets and how they are transformed.

11. Data Lineage Visualization: Utilize data lineage visualization tools to represent data flow visually. This makes it easier for data stakeholders to understand how data is used.

12. Impact Analysis: Implement impact analysis to understand how changes to data sources or transformations affect downstream data assets. This is crucial for change management and compliance.

13. Data Quality and Lineage Auditing: Regularly audit data quality and data lineage records to ensure their accuracy and completeness. Automated auditing processes can help with this.

14. Data Lineage for Compliance: Leverage data lineage records to demonstrate compliance with data regulations. Regulators may require proof of data movement and processing.

15. Data Lineage for Troubleshooting: Use data lineage information to trace issues and troubleshoot problems in your data pipeline. It can help identify bottlenecks and data inconsistencies.

By focusing on data quality and data lineage, organizations can ensure that their data is accurate, compliant, and trustworthy. This not only facilitates compliance with regulatory requirements but also enhances data-driven decision-making and boosts the overall quality of analytics and reporting.

12.2 Compliance in the Cloud

Regulatory Compliance in Azure

Ensuring regulatory compliance in the Azure cloud environment is critical, especially when handling sensitive data and applications. Azure provides a range of features and services to help organizations maintain compliance with various industry standards and regulations. In this section, we will explore best practices for achieving regulatory compliance in Azure:

1. Identify Applicable Regulations:

  - Begin by identifying the regulatory requirements that are relevant to your organization and data. This can include industry-specific standards, data privacy laws, and compliance frameworks such as GDPR, HIPAA, or SOC 2.

2. Azure Compliance Documentation:

  - Azure maintains extensive documentation related to its compliance with various industry standards. Review Azure's compliance documentation and familiarize yourself with the services that are certified for specific compliance standards.

3. Data Classification:

  - Classify your data based on sensitivity. Azure provides tools for data classification, such as Azure Information Protection, which can help you label and protect sensitive data.

4. Encryption and Data Protection:

  - Utilize Azure's encryption capabilities, including Azure Disk Encryption, Azure Storage Service Encryption, and Azure SQL Database Transparent Data Encryption (TDE) to protect data at rest and in transit.

5. Access Control and Identity Management:

- Implement Azure Active Directory (Azure AD) for identity management. Utilize role-based access control (RBAC) to manage permissions and ensure that only authorized personnel can access critical resources.

6. Compliance Assessments:

- Use Azure Policy to define and enforce organizational standards and assess compliance with those standards. Regularly evaluate compliance with these policies.

7. Audit Logging and Monitoring:

- Enable Azure Monitor and Azure Security Center to gain insights into the security and compliance status of your Azure resources. Configure audit logging for critical services.

8. Data Residency and Sovereignty:

- Be aware of data residency requirements and ensure that data is stored in Azure regions that comply with the relevant regulations. Azure provides data residency options to help you meet these requirements.

9. Azure Compliance Certifications:

- Azure holds numerous certifications and attestations, such as ISO 27001, SOC 2, and HIPAA. Understand the scope and coverage of these certifications and ensure that your usage aligns with them.

10. Compliance as Code:

- Embrace Infrastructure as Code (IaC) and configuration management tools to enforce compliance standards automatically. Tools like Azure Policy and Azure Blueprints can be used to define and enforce compliance requirements in your infrastructure code.

11. Continuous Compliance Monitoring:

- Compliance is an ongoing process. Implement continuous monitoring and reporting mechanisms to ensure that your Azure environment remains compliant with the selected standards.

12. Third-Party Compliance Tools:

- Consider using third-party compliance management tools that are compatible with Azure to streamline compliance assessments and reporting.

By following these best practices, organizations can navigate the complex landscape of regulatory compliance in Azure. Ensuring that your Azure environment complies with relevant regulations is crucial for avoiding legal and financial repercussions and maintaining trust with customers and stakeholders. Additionally, it demonstrates a commitment to data security and privacy.

Compliance with Data Privacy Laws

Ensuring compliance with data privacy laws is of paramount importance, given the increasing focus on data protection and privacy regulations globally. In this section, we will discuss best practices for achieving compliance with data privacy laws in your cloud environment, particularly when using Azure:

1. Understand Relevant Laws:

- Start by understanding the specific data privacy laws that are applicable to your organization. Laws like the General Data Protection Regulation (GDPR) in Europe, the California Consumer Privacy Act (CCPA), or others may have specific requirements for data handling.

2. Data Classification:

- Classify your data based on sensitivity and privacy requirements. This includes identifying personal data, sensitive information, and other data categories as defined by the applicable regulations.

3. Consent and Transparency:

- Implement mechanisms to obtain and manage user consent for data processing. Be transparent with users about data collection and usage, providing clear and accessible privacy policies.

4. Data Minimization:

- Collect only the data that is necessary for your business purposes. Avoid excessive data collection, which can increase compliance risks.

5. Data Encryption:

- Encrypt sensitive data at rest and in transit. Azure provides tools like Azure Information Protection, Azure Storage Service Encryption, and Azure SQL Database Transparent Data Encryption (TDE) for this purpose.

6. Data Portability:

- Ensure that users can access their data and, if required, move it to other platforms as specified in some data privacy laws like GDPR's right to data portability.

7. Data Access Controls:

- Implement strict access controls and user authentication mechanisms. Azure Active Directory (Azure AD) is a valuable tool for managing identity and access.

8. Data Deletion:

- Implement procedures to delete personal data upon request. Azure services like Azure SQL Database allow for data deletion based on defined policies.

9. Data Impact Assessments:

- Conduct Data Protection Impact Assessments (DPIAs) to assess and mitigate privacy risks. Identify and address potential privacy concerns in advance.

10. Consent and Preference Management:

- Use Azure services like Azure Logic Apps to manage user consents and preferences for data processing. This allows you to handle data in compliance with user choices.

11. Data Privacy by Design:

- Integrate privacy controls into your application design and cloud infrastructure. Follow the principles of "privacy by design" as recommended by many privacy regulations.

12. Compliance Reporting:

- Maintain records of data processing activities and regularly report on compliance efforts. Azure services like Azure Monitor can assist in tracking compliance-related events.

13. Legal Consultation:

- Depending on the complexity of your compliance requirements, it is advisable to seek legal counsel to ensure that your data handling practices align with the law.

14. Data Retention Policies:

   - Define and enforce data retention policies, ensuring data is not kept longer than necessary.

15. Data Privacy Training:

   - Train your employees about data privacy, including the regulations that apply to your organization.

By implementing these best practices, your organization can navigate the complex landscape of data privacy regulations. Complying with data privacy laws not only helps you avoid penalties but also fosters trust with your users and customers. It demonstrates your commitment to data protection and responsible data management.

Auditing and Compliance Reporting in Power BI

Ensuring compliance with regulations and internal policies is a critical aspect of data governance in a cloud environment. Power BI provides features and tools to help you audit and report on your data and dashboard usage. In this section, we will explore how to set up auditing and create compliance reports within Power BI.

1. Enabling Audit Logs in Power BI:

   - Start by enabling audit logs in Power BI to capture user and admin activities. This provides a detailed record of what is happening within your Power BI environment.

2. Activity Logging:

   - Power BI logs various activities such as report views, data source connections, dashboard interactions, and more. Activity logs can be accessed through the Power BI service.

3. Compliance Center:

- Use the Microsoft 365 Compliance Center to configure audit policies and set up alerts for specific activities. This is especially useful for tracking data access and changes.

4. Data Lineage and Impact Analysis:

- Power BI can help track the lineage of your data, showing how datasets are connected to reports and dashboards. Use data lineage to understand the impact of data changes on your reports.

5. Usage Metrics:

- Leverage Power BI's built-in usage metrics and reports to gain insights into how your reports and dashboards are being used. Understand which reports are popular and which datasets have the most views.

6. Report Versioning:

- Maintain different versions of your reports to ensure you can revert to a previous version if needed. This is especially important for compliance, as you can recover historical data.

7. Compliance Reporting:

- Generate compliance reports from the audit logs to provide visibility into who is accessing your data and reports. You can use Power BI's reporting capabilities to create custom compliance reports tailored to your organization's needs.

8. Scheduled Alerts:

- Set up alerts for specific activities or access patterns. Receive notifications when certain activities occur or when there are deviations from normal behavior.

9. Sharing and Collaboration Auditing:

- Track sharing activities within Power BI, such as sharing reports with external users, to ensure data is not being exposed to unauthorized parties.

10. User Access Auditing:

- Monitor user access to sensitive data and reports. Ensure that only authorized personnel are viewing or editing sensitive content.

11. Automated Compliance Reports:

- Automate the creation and distribution of compliance reports using Power BI's scheduled data refresh and email subscription features.

12. Data Retention Policies:

- Establish data retention policies to determine how long audit logs are kept. Be aware of any regulatory requirements regarding data retention.

13. Compliance Dashboard:

- Create a compliance dashboard that provides a real-time view of your organization's adherence to compliance policies. This dashboard can include key metrics, alerts, and trends.

By following these steps, you can establish robust auditing and compliance reporting in your Power BI environment. This not only ensures that you are following relevant regulations but also provides valuable insights into how your data and reports are being used, enabling better data governance and decision-making.

CONCLUSION

13.1 Recap of Key Takeaways

Summarizing Key Concepts

In this concluding section of the book, we will revisit the key concepts and takeaways from the preceding chapters. It's essential to recap what you've learned throughout this journey of harnessing the power of Power BI and Azure for data analytics and reporting.

1. Power BI Fundamentals:

   - Understand the core components of Power BI, including Power Query, Power Pivot, and Power View. These are the building blocks that enable data transformation, modeling, and visualization.

2. Data Preparation and Transformation:

   - Data quality is critical. Learn how to clean, transform, and shape data using Power Query to ensure it's suitable for analysis. This involves tasks like data cleansing, handling missing values, and joining multiple data sources.

3. Data Modeling:

   - Explore data modeling in Power BI using relationships, calculated columns, and measures. Proper data modeling ensures that your reports and dashboards provide accurate and meaningful insights.

4. Visualizations and Dashboards:

- Master the art of creating effective visualizations and interactive dashboards in Power BI. Understand best practices for choosing the right visuals to convey your data's story.

5. Cloud Integration:

- Embrace the cloud by integrating Power BI with Azure services. Learn how to leverage Azure Data Lake Storage, Azure SQL Data Warehouse, and other Azure resources for robust data analytics.

6. Real-World Use Cases:

- Explore practical case studies that illustrate how Power BI and Azure are applied to solve real-world business problems. These case studies offer valuable insights into the integration of technologies in a business context.

7. Data Governance and Compliance:

- Delve into the importance of data governance and compliance. Understand how to establish data governance policies, manage metadata, ensure data quality, and meet regulatory compliance requirements.

8. Troubleshooting and Maintenance:

- Gain insights into troubleshooting common issues, diagnosing data connection problems, debugging performance, and handling security and access problems.

9. The Value of Integration:

- Finally, recognize the value of integrating Power BI and Azure. The synergy between these tools empowers organizations to achieve comprehensive data analytics, improved decision-making, and enhanced data governance.

By summarizing these key concepts, you'll have a clear understanding of the essential elements required to master Power BI and Azure integration for data analytics and reporting. The synergy between these technologies opens up a world of possibilities for organizations seeking to derive insights from their data, make informed decisions, and remain compliant with data regulations.

The Value of Integration

In this final chapter, we explore the immense value that integration of Power BI and Azure brings to your data analytics and reporting efforts. This synergy creates a powerful ecosystem for handling, analyzing, and visualizing data, and it provides numerous benefits:

1. Scalability: Azure's cloud resources enable you to handle massive datasets and growing workloads. Whether you need to analyze historical data or perform real-time analytics, Azure's scalability ensures your system can adapt to the changing needs of your organization.

2. Data Security and Compliance: Azure offers robust security features and compliance certifications, ensuring your data is protected, and you meet regulatory requirements. This is crucial, especially when dealing with sensitive data or data subject to industry-specific regulations like HIPAA or GDPR.

3. Seamless Data Flow: Azure Data Factory allows you to create data pipelines that can automate the flow of data between various sources and Power BI. This streamlines the process of data collection, transformation, and reporting, saving time and reducing errors.

4. Real-time Insights: Integration with Azure Stream Analytics enables real-time data processing and analytics. This is invaluable when you need to monitor live data streams or respond to critical events as they happen.

5. Centralized Data Management: Azure Data Lake Storage and other Azure services provide a centralized and scalable repository for your data. This centralization simplifies data management, making it easier to access, update, and maintain your data.

6. Advanced Analytics: Azure Machine Learning integration with Power BI allows for advanced analytics and predictive modeling. You can build machine learning models and incorporate them directly into your reports and dashboards.

7. Cost Efficiency: Azure's pay-as-you-go pricing model means you only pay for the resources you use. This cost efficiency can significantly reduce your operational expenses compared to maintaining on-premises infrastructure.

8. Integration of Diverse Data Sources: Azure supports a wide variety of data sources, making it possible to integrate data from different systems, databases, and file formats into your Power BI reports.

9. Enhanced Collaboration: With Azure and Power BI integrated, collaboration among team members is simplified. Everyone can work on the same datasets, models, and reports, leading to more efficient teamwork.

10. Future-Proofing: By adopting Azure and Power BI, you're investing in technologies that are continuously evolving. Microsoft consistently releases updates and new features, ensuring your analytics capabilities stay current and competitive.

In summary, the integration of Power BI and Azure provides a holistic solution for organizations seeking to harness the full potential of their data. The benefits of scalability, security, real-time insights, centralized data management, advanced analytics, cost efficiency, and more make this combination a game-changer for data analytics and reporting. As the data landscape continues to evolve, this integrated approach positions you to thrive in the data-driven future.

13.2 Future Trends in Cloud Analytics with Power BI and Azure

The Evolving Landscape of Cloud Analytics

As we look to the future, the landscape of cloud analytics with Power BI and Azure is poised for exciting developments and transformations. Several trends and changes are expected to shape the way organizations handle their data, analytics, and reporting. Understanding these trends is essential for staying competitive in the data-driven world. Let's explore some of the key aspects of the evolving cloud analytics landscape:

1. Artificial Intelligence and Machine Learning Integration: AI and ML will continue to play a pivotal role in cloud analytics. We can expect more seamless integration of AI and ML capabilities into Power BI and Azure services. This will empower organizations to gain deeper insights, predict future trends, and automate decision-making processes.

2. Augmented Analytics: Augmented analytics will become more prevalent, enabling business users to uncover insights and generate reports without extensive data analysis expertise. Natural language processing, automated insights, and smart recommendations will become standard features in analytics tools.

3. Data Governance and Compliance: With the increasing importance of data privacy regulations (e.g., GDPR, CCPA), data governance and compliance will remain a top priority. Organizations will focus on ensuring that their data handling practices meet regulatory requirements, and tools like Power BI and Azure will provide enhanced features for data cataloging, lineage, and auditing.

4. Real-time Analytics: Real-time data processing and analytics will continue to gain prominence. More businesses will require instant access to critical information, and the

integration of real-time data sources with Power BI will enable decision-makers to act swiftly based on the freshest data.

5. Edge Analytics: Edge computing and analytics will expand as IoT devices generate vast amounts of data at the source. Azure services will facilitate edge analytics, allowing organizations to process and analyze data locally before transmitting relevant insights to the cloud.

6. Hybrid Cloud Solutions: Many organizations will adopt a hybrid cloud approach, combining on-premises, private cloud, and public cloud environments. Power BI and Azure will offer seamless hybrid solutions for data management and analytics.

7. Data Storytelling: Data storytelling will become an essential skill in analytics. The ability to convey insights and findings through compelling narratives will be highly valued. Power BI's capabilities for creating data stories will evolve to support this trend.

8. Customization and Self-Service Analytics: Customization of reports and dashboards, along with self-service analytics, will become more accessible. Power BI will offer enhanced tools for designing engaging and interactive reports, and users will be able to customize their analytics experiences to suit their specific needs.

9. Serverless and Pay-as-You-Go Models: The trend of serverless computing and pay-as-you-go pricing models will continue. Organizations will appreciate the flexibility and cost-efficiency of these models, ensuring that they only pay for the resources they consume.

10. Ecosystem Expansions: The Power BI and Azure ecosystem will continue to expand with new services and integrations. Microsoft's commitment to innovation means that users can expect regular updates and enhancements.

In preparing for future developments, organizations should stay agile, adapt to new technologies, invest in employee training, and prioritize data security and governance. Keeping up with these trends will ensure that your analytics and reporting capabilities remain at the forefront of the industry, enabling data-driven decisions and continued success.

Preparing for Future Developments

As the world of cloud analytics with Power BI and Azure continues to evolve, organizations must proactively prepare for future developments to maintain a competitive edge and make the most of emerging opportunities. Here, we will outline a practical roadmap for preparing your organization to embrace upcoming trends and innovations:

1. Stay Informed and Educated:

- Encourage continuous learning among your team. Ensure that data professionals, analysts, and decision-makers are aware of the latest trends and developments in cloud analytics.

- Invest in training and upskilling programs to equip your staff with the necessary skills to work with cutting-edge technologies.

2. Data Governance and Compliance:

- Strengthen your organization's commitment to data governance and compliance. Regularly audit data handling practices to ensure alignment with evolving data privacy regulations.

- Implement robust data cataloging, metadata management, and data lineage solutions to support compliance and enhance data quality.

3. Cloud Integration Strategy:

- Develop or refine your cloud integration strategy. Consider a hybrid cloud approach that allows you to leverage both on-premises and cloud resources as needed.

- Evaluate the evolving landscape of Azure services and determine how they can best support your business goals.

4. AI and Machine Learning:

- Embrace AI and machine learning as integral components of your analytics ecosystem. Explore how AI-driven insights can drive business value.

- Collaborate with data scientists to build and deploy machine learning models that provide predictive and prescriptive analytics.

5. Real-time Analytics:

- Assess your need for real-time analytics. Identify areas in your business where real-time data can make a significant impact and work on integrating real-time data sources with your analytics tools.

- Create or fine-tune your data streaming and processing architecture.

6. Edge Analytics:

- If your organization uses or plans to use IoT devices, investigate edge analytics solutions. Develop the infrastructure needed for edge data processing and analyze data locally before transmitting it to the cloud.

7. Customization and Self-Service:

- Promote the culture of self-service analytics within your organization. Invest in tools and training that empower business users to create their own reports and dashboards.

- Encourage data storytelling and the sharing of insights through compelling narratives.

8. Cost Optimization:

- Continually assess your cloud resources to ensure cost optimization. Opt for serverless and pay-as-you-go models when appropriate.

- Leverage tools and best practices to monitor resource usage and costs.

9. Ecosystem Expansion:

- Keep an eye on the growth of the Power BI and Azure ecosystem. Regularly update your tools and consider integrating new services that align with your business objectives.

10. Agility and Adaptability:

- Foster an agile and adaptable culture. Ensure your organization can quickly pivot to take advantage of new opportunities and address emerging challenges.

- Develop change management strategies to facilitate the adoption of new technologies and practices.

11. Future-Proofing Your Data Architecture:

- Build a data architecture that is scalable and flexible, capable of accommodating new data sources and technologies.

- Consider the potential migration to modern data warehouses or data lakes for improved data management and analytics capabilities.

12. Collaboration and Communication:

- Promote collaboration between IT and business units. Encourage a shared vision and understanding of the role of analytics in driving business success.

- Establish clear communication channels for sharing insights and findings derived from data analytics.

13. User Feedback and Adoption:

   - Gather feedback from users regularly. Use their input to fine-tune your analytics solutions and improve user adoption.

   - Foster a culture of data-driven decision-making and ensure that analytics insights influence strategic planning.

By taking these steps and continually reassessing your approach to cloud analytics, you'll be well-prepared to navigate the evolving landscape of data and technology. Stay agile, invest in skills and resources, and adapt to change. This will position your organization for success in the future of cloud analytics with Power BI and Azure.

Dear Valued Reader,

We extend our heartfelt gratitude to you for choosing "Power BI and Azure: Integrating Cloud Analytics for Scalable Solutions." Your decision to purchase this book is greatly appreciated, and we sincerely hope it proves to be an invaluable resource on your journey to mastering the world of cloud analytics with Power BI and Azure.

This book has been meticulously crafted to provide you with practical insights, detailed guidance, and real-world use cases, all aimed at empowering you to harness the full potential of your data. Whether you're a novice or an experienced professional, the knowledge and skills you'll acquire from this book will undoubtedly enhance your ability to make data-driven decisions and excel in your analytical endeavors.

Thank you for entrusting us with your learning and development. We are committed to supporting you in your quest to become a proficient cloud analytics practitioner. Your satisfaction and success are our ultimate goals.

Please don't hesitate to reach out with any questions or feedback. We value your input and strive to continuously improve to meet your evolving needs.

Once again, thank you for choosing "Power BI and Azure: Integrating Cloud Analytics for Scalable Solutions." We wish you a rewarding and enlightening reading experience.

Sincerely,